D0040750

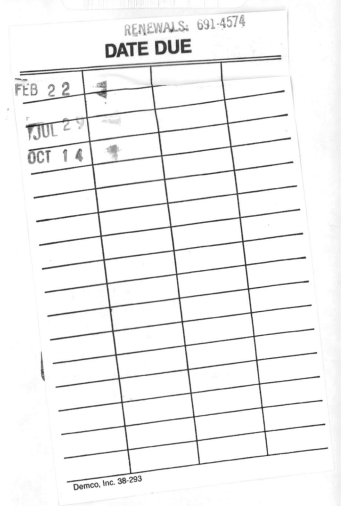

ONE ARM

# By TENNESSEE WILLIAMS

PLAYS

Baby Doll (a screenplay)
Cat on a Hot Tin Roof
   (American Shakespeare Theatre Production)
Camino Real
Dragon Country
The Glass Menagerie
A Lovely Sunday for Creve Couer
Small Craft Warnings
Sweet Bird of Youth
A Streetcar Named Desire
THE THEATRE OF TENNESSEE WILLIAMS
   VOLUME I: *Battle of Angels, A Streetcar
   Named Desire, The Glass Menagerie*
   VOLUME II: *The Eccentricities of a Nightingale,
   Summer and Smoke, The Rose Tattoo, Camino Real*
   VOLUME III: *Cat on a Hot Tin Roof, Orpheus
   Descending, Suddenly Last Summer*
   VOLUME IV: *Sweet Bird of Youth, Period of Ad-
   justment, The Night of the Iguana*
   VOLUME V: *The Milk Train Doesn't Stop Here Any-
   more, Kingdom of Earth (The Seven Descents of
   Myrtle), Small Craft Warnings, The Two-Character
   Play*
27 Wagons Full of Cotton
The Two-Character Play
Vieux Carré

POETRY

Androgyne, Mon Amour
In the Winter of Cities

PROSE

Eight Mortal Ladies Possessed
Hard Candy and Other Stories
The Knightly Quest and Other Stories
One Arm and Other Stories
The Roman Spring of Mrs. Stone
Where I Live (selected essays)

TENNESSEE WILLIAMS

# ONE ARM

*AND OTHER STORIES*

*A NEW DIRECTIONS BOOK*

Library of Congress catalog card number: 57-31974
ISBN: 0-8112-0223-2
First published by New Directions in 1948.
Revised edition, 1957.
First ND paperback edition, 1967.
Published in Canada by George J. McLeod, Ltd., Toronto

New Directions Books are published for James Laughlin
by New Directions Publishing Corporation,
80 Eighth Avenue, New York 10011

SIXTH PRINTING

TO THE MEMORY
OF KIP

# CONTENTS

# ONE ARM

Iɴ New Orleans in the winter of '39 there were three male hustlers usually to be found hanging out on a certain corner of Canal Street and one of those streets that dive narrowly into the ancient part of the city. Two of them were just kids of about seventeen and worth only passing attention, but the oldest of the three was an unforgettable youth. His name was Oliver Winemiller and he had been the light heavyweight champion boxer of the Pacific fleet before he lost an arm. Now he looked like a broken statue of Apollo, and he had also the coolness and impassivity of a stone figure.

While the two younger boys exhibited the anxious energy of sparrows, darting in and out of bars, flitting across streets and around corners in pursuit of some likely quarry, Oliver would remain in one spot and wait to be spoken to. He never spoke first, nor solicited with a look. He seemed to be staring above the heads of passers-by with an indifference which was not put on, or surly and vain, but had its root in a genuine lack of concern. He paid almost no attention to weather. When the cold rains swept in from the Gulf the two younger boys stood hunched and shuddering in shabby coats that effaced them altogether. But Oliver remained in his skivvy shirt and his dungarees which had faded nearly white from long wear and much washing, and held to his body as smooth as the clothes of sculpture.

Conversations like this would occur on the corner.

"Aren't you afraid of catching cold, young fellow?"

"No, I don't catch cold."

"Well, there's a first time for everything."

"Sure is."

"You ought to go in somewhere and get warmed up."

"Where?"

"I have an apartment."

"Which way is it?"

"A few blocks down in the Quarter. We'll take a cab."

"Let's walk and you give me the cab-fare."

Oliver had been in his crippled condition for just two years. The injury had been suffered in the seaport of San Diego when he and a group of shipmates had collided with the wall of an underpass while driving a rented car at seventy-five miles an hour. Two of the sailors in the car had been killed outright, a third had received a spinal

8

injury that would keep him in a wheel chair for the rest of his life. Oliver got off lightest with just the loss of an arm. He was eighteen then and his experience had been limited. He came from the cotton fields of Arkansas, where he had known only hard work in the sun and such emotional adventures as farm boys have on Saturday nights and Sunday afternoons, a tentative knowledge of girls that suddenly exploded into a coarse and startling affair with a married woman whose husband he had hauled lumber for. She was the first to make him aware of the uncommon excitement he was able to stir. It was to break off this affair that he left home and entered the navy at a base in Texas. During his period of training he had taken up boxing and while he was still a 'boot' he became an outstanding contender for the navy championship. The life was good fun and no thinking. All that he had to deal with was the flesh and its feelings. But then the arm had been lost, and with it he was abruptly cut off from his development as an athlete and a young man wholly adequate to the physical world he grew into.

Oliver couldn't have put into words the psychic change which came with his mutilation. He knew that he had lost his right arm, but didn't consciously know that with it had gone the center of his being. But the self that doesn't form words nor even thoughts had come to a realization that whirled darkly up from its hidden laboratory and changed him altogether in less time than it took new skin to cover the stump of the arm he had lost. He never said to himself, I'm lost. But the speechless self knew it and in submission to its unthinking control the youth had begun as soon as he left the hospital to look about for destruction.

He took to knocking about the country, going first to New York. It was there that Oliver learned the ropes of what became his calling. He fell in with another young vagrant who wised him up to his commodity value and how to cash in on it. Within a week the one-armed youth was fully inured to the practices and the culture of the underworld that seethed around Times Square and the Broadway bars and the bench-lined walks of the park, and foreign as it was, the shock that it gave him was slight. The loss of the arm had apparently dulled his senses. With it had gone the wholesome propriety that had made him leave home when the coarse older woman had introduced him to acts of unnatural ardor. Now he could feel no shame that green soap and water did not remove well enough to satisfy him.

When summer had passed, he joined the southern migration. He lived in Miami a while. He struck it rich down there. He made the acquaintance of some wealthy sportsmen and all that season he passed from one to another with money that piled up faster than he could spend it on clothes and amusement. Then one night he got drunk on a broker's yacht in the harbor at Palm Beach and, for no reason that was afterward sure to him, he struck the man's inclined head eight times with a copper book-end, the final stroke splitting the skull. He swam to shore, collected his things and beat it out of the State. This ended the more affluent chapter of

Oliver's existence. From that time on he moved for protection in less conspicuous channels, losing himself in the swarm of his fugitive kind wherever a town was large enough for such traffic to pass without too much attention.

Then, one evening during this winter in New Orleans, shortly after the Mardi Gras season and when he was beginning to think of heading back North, Oliver was picked up by a plain-clothesman and driven to jail, not on an ordinary charge of lewd vagrancy, but for questioning in connection with the murder of the wealthy broker in the harbor at Palm Beach. They got a full confession from him in fifteen minutes.

He hardly made any effort to dodge their questions.

They gave him half a tumbler of whiskey to loosen his tongue and he gave them a lurid account of the party the broker had given on his yacht. Oliver and a girl prostitute had been given a hundred dollars each to perform in what is called a blue movie, that is, a privately made film of licentious behavior among two or more persons, usually with some crude sort of narrative sequence. He and the girl had undressed by drunken stages before the camera and the yacht party, and had gone through a sequence of such embraces and intimacies as only four walls and a locked door usually witness. The film was not finished. To his own astonishment, Oliver had suddenly revolted, struck the girl and kicked the camera over and fled to the upper deck. Up there he had guessed that if he remained on the yacht he would do something still more violent. But when the others finally went ashore in a launch, Oliver had remained because the host had wheedled him with money and the promise of more.

"I knew when they left him alone with me that he would be sorry," Oliver said in his statement to the police. It was this admission which the prosecutor used to establish premeditation in the case.

Everything went against him at the trial. His testimony was ineffectual against the prestige of the other witnesses, all of whom swore that nothing irregular had occurred on the yacht. [No one remembered anything about the blue movie except Oliver, the girl prostitute was equally unheard of.] And the fact that Oliver had removed from the victim's body a diamond ring and a wallet assured the youth's conviction and doomed him to the chair.

The arrest of the broker's killer was given space in papers all over the country. The face of the one-armed youth was shot from newspapers into the startled eyes of men who had known him in all those places Oliver had passed through in his aimless travels. None of these men who had known him had found his image one that faded readily out of mind. The great blond youth who had been a boxer until he had lost an arm had stood as a planet among the moons of their longing, fixed in his orbit while they circled about him. Now he was caught somewhere, he had crashed into ruin. And in a sense this ruin had returned him to them. He was no longer on highways or tracks going further, but penned in a corner and waiting only for death.

He began to receive letters from them. Each morning the jailor thrust more envelopes through the bars of his cell. The letters were usually signed by fictitious names and if they requested an answer, the address given would be general delivery in one of those larger cities where Oliver's calling was plied. They were written on fine white paper, some of them were faintly scented, and some enclosed paper money. The messages were similarly phrased. All of them spoke of their shock at his dilemma, they couldn't believe it was true, it was like a bad dream, and so forth. They made allusions to the nights which he had spent with them, or the few hours which they almost invariably pronounced to be the richest of their entire experience. There was something about him, they wrote, not only the physical thing, important as that was, which had made him haunt their minds since.

What they were alluding to was the charm of the defeated which Oliver had possessed, a quality which acts as a poultice upon the inflamed nerves of those who are still in active contention. This quality is seldom linked with youth and physical charm, but in Oliver's case it had been, and it was this rare combination which had made him a person impossible to forget. And because he was sentenced to death, Oliver had for these correspondents the curtained and abstract quality of the priest who listens without being visible to confessions of guilt. The usual restraints upon the unconscious were accordingly lifted and the dark joys of *mea culpa* were freely indulged in. The litanies of their sorrows were poured onto paper like water from broken dams. To some he became the archetype of the Savior Upon The Cross who had taken upon himself the sins of their world to be washed and purified in his blood and passion. Letters of this sort enraged the imprisoned boy and he clamped them under one foot and tore them to pieces and tossed the pieces in his slop bucket.

With the mechanical cruelty of the law, the execution of Oliver's sentence had given him several months in which to expect it and they were the months of summer. In his stifling cubicle there was very little to do while waiting for death and time enough with the impetus of disaster for the boy's malleable nature to be remoulded still again, and the instrument of this process became the letters.

He sat on a folding chair or sprawled on his cot those first few weeks in the death house in a way that was not unlike the way in which he had stood against a brick-wall in rain-soaked dungarees and skivvy shirt on the New Orleans corner till someone had asked him for the time or a light. He was given a deck of cards with stains of candy bars on them and tattered books of comic and adventure cartoons to pass away time with. And there was a radio at the end of the corridor. But Oliver was cut off from the world that blared through the mouth of the radio and from that world of one-dimensional clownery and heroism in the raw colors of childhood's spectrum which the cartoon strips celebrated. All of these rushed by him instead of with him, and only the letters remained in connection with him.

After a while he not only read all of the letters, but folded them back in their envelopes and began to accumulate them in rubber bands on a shelf. One night without thinking he took them down from the shelf and placed them beneath his pillow, and he went to sleep with his one hand resting on them.

A few weeks before the time for his execution Oliver began to write out replies to those men who had begged to hear from him. He used a soft lead pencil that dwindled rapidly to a stub beneath his awkward pressure. He wrote on manila paper and mailed the replies in government stamped envelopes to all of those cities that he had formerly haunted.

Having had no surviving family to write to, this was Oliver's first attempt at writing letters. He wrote at first with a laborious stiffness. The composition of the simplest sentence would knot up the muscles in his one powerful arm, but as the writing went on a greater laxity developed in a wonderfully short time. Soon the sentences gathered momentum as springs that clear out a channel and they began to flow out almost expressively after a while and to ring with the crudely eloquent backwoods speech of the South, to which had been added salty idioms of the underworld he had moved in, and the road, and the sea. Into them went the warm and vivid talk that liquor and generous dealing had brought from his lips on certain occasions, the *chansons de geste* which American tongues throw away so casually in bars and hotel bedrooms. The cartoon symbol of laughter was often employed, that heavily drawn HA-HA with its tail of exclamatory punctuation, its stars and spirals, and setting that down on paper was what gave him most relief, for it had the feel of the boiling intensity in him. He would often include a rough illustration, a sketch of the chair that he was condemned to sit in.

The letters would go like this.

"Yes, I remember you plainly. I met you in the park in back of the public library, or was it the men's room in the Greyhound depot. I met so many they sometimes get mixed up. However you stand out plainly. You asked for the time or a light and we got to talking and first thing I knew we was in your apartment drinking. And how is Chicago now that it's summer again? I sure would appreciate feeling those cool lake breezes or pouring down shots of that wonderful Five Star Connyack where we shacked up that day. I tell you it's hot in this cooler. Cooler is good. Ha-ha! One thing I can sure count on is it's going to get hotter before it gets cooler again. If you get what I mean. I mean the chair on the wire that is patiently waiting for me to sit down in it. The date is the tenth of August and you are invited except that you could not get in. It is very exclusive. I guess you would like to know if I am afraid. The answer is Yes. I do not look forward to it. I was a boxer until I lost my arm and after that happened I seemed to go through a change which I cannot account for except I was very disgusted with all of the world. I guess I stopped caring about what happened to me. That is to say I had lost my self-respect.

"I went all over the country without any plans except to keep on moving. I picked up strangers in every city I went to. I had experience with them which only meant money to me and a place to shack up for the night and liquor and food. I never thought it could mean very much to them. Now all of these letters like yours have proven it did. I meant something very important to hundreds of people whose faces and names had slipped clean out my mind as soon as I left them. I feel as if I had run up a debt of some kind. Not money but feelings. I treated some of them badly. Went off without even so much as saying goodbye in spite of all their generosity to me and even took things which hadn't been given to me. I cannot imagine how some of these men could forgive me. If I had known then, I mean when I was outside, that such true feelings could even be found in strangers, I mean of the kind that I picked up for a living, I guess I might have felt there was more to live for. Anyhow now the situation is hopeless. All will be over for me in a very short while. Ha-ha!

"You probably didn't know that I was an artist as well as being a one-armed champion boxer and therefore I'm going to draw you a wonderful picture!"

This writing of letters became his one occupation, and as a stone gathers heat when lain among coals, the doomed man's brain grew warmer and warmer with a sense of communion. Coming prior to disaster, this change might have been a salvation. It might have offered a center for personal integration which the boy had not had since the mandala dream of the prize ring had gone with the arm. A personality without a center throws up a wall and lives in a state of siege. So Oliver had cultivated his cold and absolute insularity behind which had lain the ruined city of the crippled champion. Within those battlements had been little or nothing to put up a fight for survival. Now something was stirring within.

But this coming to life was unmerciful, coming so late. The indifference had passed off when it should have remained to make death easier for him. And time passed quicker. In the changeless enclosure of his cell the time that stood between the youth and his death wore away like the soft lead pencil that he wrote with, until only a stub too small for his grasp was left him.

But how alive he still was!

Before imprisonment he had thought of his maimed body as something that, being broken, was only fit for abuse. You God-damned cripple, he used to groan to himself. The excitement he stirred in others had been incomprehensible and disgusting to him. But lately the torrent of letters from men whom he had forgotten who couldn't stop thinking of him had begun to revive his self-interest. Auto-erotic sensations began to flower in him. He felt the sorrowful pleasure that stirred his groin in response to manipulation. Lying nude on the cot in the southern July, his one large hand made joyless love to his body, exploring all of those erogenous zones that the fingers of others, hundreds of stranger's fingers, had clasped with a hunger that now was beginning to be understandable to him. Too late, this resurrection. Better for all those rainbows of the flesh to have stayed with the arm cut off in San Diego.

During the earlier period of his confinement Oliver had not particularly noticed or cared about the spatial limitations of his cell. Then he had been satisfied to sit on the edge of his cot and move no more than was necessary for bodily functions. That had been merciful. However, it was now gone and every morning he seemed to wake up in a space that had mysteriously diminished while he slept. The inner repressions took this way of screaming for their release. The restlessness became a phobia and the phobia was turning into panic.

He could not remain still for a moment. His heavy foot pads sounded from the end of the hall like an ape's, for he walked barefooted with rapid, shuffling strides around and around the little space of his cage. He talked to himself in a monotonous undertone that grew louder, as the days passed, until it began to compete with the endless chatter and blare of the guards' radio. At first he would hush up when he was ordered to, but later his panic deafened him to the guards' voices, until they shouted threats at him. Then he would grip the bars of his cage door and shout back at them names and curses more violent than their own. The doomed boy's behavior cut off whatever acts of humanity these hard men might have shown him as he drew close to his death. Finally, on the third day before his execution, they punished one of his tantrums by turning the fire-hose on him, until he was crushed to the floor in a strangling heap. He lay there and sobbed and cursed with his brain spinning through a dizzy spiral of nightmares.

By this time, the writing of letters was altogether cut off, but during his quieter intervals he drew wild pictures in his manila tablet and printed out the violent comic-strip symbols, especially the immense HA-HA with its screaming punctuation. Sedatives were put in his food in the last few days, but the drugs were burned up in the furnace of his nerves and the little sleep they gave him would plunge him in worse nightmares than the ones of waking.

The day before he would die Oliver received a visitor in the death cell.

The visitor was a young Lutheran minister who had just come out of the seminary and had not yet received an appointment to a church. Oliver had refused to see the prison chaplain. This had been mentioned in the local newspapers with a picture of Oliver and a caption, Condemned Youth Refuses Consolation of Faith. It had spoken also of the hard and unrepentant nature of the boy who was to die very soon and of his violent behavior in the prison. But the picture was incongruous to these facts, the face of the blond youth having a virile but tender beauty of the sort that some painter of the Renaissance might have slyly attributed to a juvenile saint, a look which had sometimes inspired commentators to call him "the baby-faced killer."

From the moment that he had seen this photograph the Lutheran minister had been following out a series of compulsions so strong that he appeared to himself to be surrendering to an outside power. His earnestness was so apparent that he had no trouble convincing the warden that his mission to the youth was divinely inspired, but by the time the pass was issued, the force of his compulsions had so exhausted the young minister that he fell into a state of nervous panic and would have fled from the building if he had not been attended by a guard.

He found Oliver seated on the edge of his cot senselessly rubbing the sole of a bare foot. He wore only a pair of shorts and his sweating body radiated a warmth that struck the visitor like a powerful spotlight. The appearance of the boy had not been falsely reported. At his first swift glance the minister's mind shot back to an obsession of his childhood when he had gone all of one summer daily to the zoo to look at a golden panther. The animal was supposed to be particularly savage and a sign on its cage had admonished visitors to keep their distance. But the look in the animal's eyes was so radiant with innocence that the child, who was very timid and harassed by reasonless anxieties, had found a mysterious comfort in meeting their gaze and had come to see them staring benignly out of the darkness when his own eyes were closed before sleeping. Then he would cry himself to sleep for pity of the animal's imprisonment and an unfathomable longing that moved through all of his body.

But one night he dreamed of the panther in a shameful way. The immense clear eyes had appeared to him in a forest and he had thought, if I lie down very quietly the panther will come near me and I am not afraid of him because of our long communions through the bars. He took off his clothes before lying down in the forest. A chill wind began to stir and he felt himself shivering. Then a little fear started in his nerves. He began to doubt his security with the panther and he was afraid to open his eyes again, but he reached out and slowly and noiselessly as possible gathered some leaves about his shuddering nudity and lay under them in a tightly curled position trying to breathe as softly as possible and hoping that now the panther would not discover him. But the chill little wind grew stronger and the leaves blew away. Then all at once he was warm in spite of the windy darkness about him and he realized that the warmth was that of the golden panther coming near him. It was no longer any use trying to conceal himself and it was too late to make an attempt at flight, and so with a sigh the dreamer uncurled his body from its tight position and lay outstretched and spread-eagled in an attitude of absolute trust and submission. Something began to stroke him and presently because of its liquid heat he realized that it was the tongue of the beast bathing him as such animals bathe their young, starting at his feet but progressing slowly up the length of his legs until the narcotic touch arrived at his loins, and then the dream had taken the shameful turn and he had awakened burning with shame beneath the damp and aching initial of Eros.

He had visited the golden panther only once after that and had found himself unable to meet the radiant scrutiny of the beast without mortification. And so the idyl had ended, or had seemed to end. But here was the look of the golden panther again, the innocence in the danger, an exact parallel so unmistakably clear that the minister knew it and felt the childish instinct to curl into a protective circle and cover his body with leaves.

Instead, he reached into his pocket and took out a box of tablets.

The very clear gaze of the boy was now fixed on him, but neither of them had spoken and the guard had closed the door of the cell and withdrawn to his station at the end of the corridor, which was out of their sight.

"What is that?" asked the boy.

"Barbital tablets. I am not very well," the minister whispered.

"What is the matter with you?"

"A little functional trouble of the heart."

He had put the tablet on his tongue, but the tongue was utterly dry. He could not swallow.

"Water?" he whispered.

Oliver got up and went to the tap. He filled an enamelled tin cup with tepid water and handed it to his caller.

"What have you come here for?" he asked the young man.

"Just for a talk."

"I have got nothing to say but the deal is rugged."

"Then let me read something to you?"

"What's something?"

"The twenty-first Psalm."

"I told them I didn't want no chaplain in here."

"I am not the chaplain, I am just—"

"Just what?"

"A stranger with sympathy for the misunderstood."

Oliver shrugged and went on rubbing the sole of his foot. The minister sighed and coughed.

"Are you prepared," he whispered.

"I'm not prepared for the hot seat, if that's what you mean. But the seat is prepared for me, so what is the difference?"

"I am talking about Eternity," said the minister.

"This world of ours, this transitory existence, is just a threshold to something Immense beyond."

"Bull," said Oliver.

"You don't believe me?"

"Why should I?"

"Because you are face to face with the last adventure!"

This answer had shot from his tongue with a sort of exultant power. He was embarrassed by the boy's steady look. He turned away from it as he finally had from the golden panther's the last time he had gone to him.

"Ha-ha!" said Oliver.

"I'm only trying to help you to realize—"

Oliver cut in.

"I was a boxer. I lost my arm. Why was that?"

"Because you persisted in error."

"Bull," said Oliver. "I was not the driver of the car. I yelled at the son of a bitch, slow down, you fucker. Then came the crash. A boxer, my arm comes off. Explain that to me."

"It gave you the chance of a lifetime."

"A chance for what?"

"To grow your spiritual arms and reach for God." He leaned toward Oliver and gripped the prisoner's knees. "Don't think of me as a man, but as a connection!"

"Huh?"

"A wire that is plugged in your heart and charged with a message from God."

The curiously ambient look of the condemned youth was fixed on his visitor's face for several seconds.

Then he said, "Wet that towel."

"What towel?"

"The one that is over the chair you're sitting in."

"It's not very clean."

"I guess it is clean enough to use on Ollie."

"What do you want to do with it?"

"Rub the sweat off my back."

The minister dampened the crumpled and stiffened cloth and handed it to the boy.

"You do it for me."

"Do what?"

"Rub the sweat off my back."

He rolled on his stomach with a long-drawn sigh, an exhalation that brought again to his frightened visitor's mind the golden panther of fifteen years ago. The rubbing went on for a minute.

"Do I smell?" asked Oliver.

"No. Why?"

"I am clean," said the boy. "I took a bath after breakfast."

"Yes."

"I have always been careful to keep myself clean. I was a very clean fighter — and a very clean whore!"

He said, "Ha-ha! Did you know that I was a whore?"

"No," said the other.

"Well, that's what I was all right. That was my second profession."

The rubbing continued for another minute, during which an invisible drummer had seemed to the minister to be advancing from the end of the corridor to the door

26

of the cell and then to come through the bars and stand directly above them.

It was his heartbeat. Now it was becoming irregular and his breath whistled. He dropped the towel and dug in his white shirt pocket for the box of sedatives, but when he removed it he found that the cardboard was pulpy with sweat and the tablets had oozed together in a white paste.

"Go on," said Oliver. "It feels good."

He arched his body and pulled his shorts further down. The narrow and sculptural flanks of the youth were exposed.

"Now," said Oliver softly, "rub with your hands."

The Lutheran sprang from the cot.

"No!"

"Don't be a fool. There's a door at the end of the hall. It makes a noise when anybody comes in it."

The minister retreated.

The boy reached out and caught him by the wrist.

"You see that pile of letters on the shelf? They're bills from people I owe. Not money, but feelings. For three whole years I went all over the country stirring up feelings without feeling nothing myself. Now that's all changed and I have feelings, too. I am lonely and bottled up the same as you are. I know your type. Everything is artistic or else it's religious, but that's all a bunch of bullshit and I don't buy it. All that you need's to be given a push on the head!"

He moved toward the man as if he would give him the push.

The caller cried out. The guard came running to let him out of the cell. He had to be lifted and half carried down the corridor and before he had reached the end of it, he started to retch as if his whole insides were being torn out.

Oliver heard him.

"Maybe he'll come back tonight," the doomed boy thought. But he didn't come back and then Oliver died with all of his debts unpaid. However, he died with a good deal more dignity than he had given his jailors to expect of him.

During the last few hours his attention returned to the letters. He read them over and over, whispering them aloud. And when the warden came to conduct him to the death chamber, he said, "I would like to take these here along with me." He carried them into the death chamber with him as a child takes a doll or a toy into a dentist's office to give the protection of the familiar and loved.

The letters were resting companionably in the fork of his thighs when he sat down in the chair. At the last moment a guard reached out to remove them. But Oliver's thighs closed on them in a desperate vise that could not have been easily broken. The warden gave a signal to let them remain. Then the moment came, the atmosphere hummed and darkened. Bolts from across the frontiers of the unknown, the practically named and employed but illimitably mysterious power that first invested a static infinitude of space with heat and brilliance and motion, were channeled through Oliver's nerve cells

28

for an instant and then shot back across those immense frontiers, having claimed and withdrawn whatever was theirs in the boy whose lost right arm had been known as "lightning in leather."

The body, unclaimed after death, was turned over to a medical college to be used in a class room laboratory. The men who performed the dissection were somewhat abashed by the body under their knives. It seemed intended for some more august purpose, to stand in a gallery of antique sculpture, touched only by light through stillness and contemplation, for it had the nobility of some broken Apollo that no one was likely to carve so purely again.

But death has never been much in the way of completion.

# THE MALEDICTION

# THE

# MALEDICTION

**W**HEN a panicky little man looks for a place to stay in an unknown town, the counter-magic of learning abruptly deserts him. The demon spirits that haunted a primitive world are called back out of exile. Slyly, triumphantly, then, they creep once more through the secret pores of rocks and veins of wood that knowledge had forced them out of. The lonely stranger, scared of his shadow and shocked by the sound of his footsteps, marches through watchful ranks of lesser deities with dark intentions. He does not look at houses as much as they look at him. Streets have an attitude toward him. Sign-posts, windows, doorways all have eyes and mouths that observe him and whisper about him. The tension in him coils up tighter and tighter. If someone smiles to offer a sudden welcome, this simple act may set off a kind of explosion. The skin of his body, as cramped as a new kid glove, may seem to be split down the seams, releasing his spirit to kiss stone walls and dance over distant roof-tops. The demons are once more dispersed, thrust back into limbo; the earth is quiet and docile and mindless again, a dull-witted ox that moves in a circular furrow, to plow up sections of time for man's convenience.

This was, in fact, the way that Lucio felt when he first encountered his future companion, the cat. She was the first living-creature in all of the strange northern city that seemed to answer the asking look in his eyes. She looked back at him with cordial recognition. Almost he could hear the cat pronouncing his name. "Oh, so it's *you, Lucio!*" she seemed to be saying, "I've sat here waiting for you a long, long time!"

Lucio smiled in return and went on up to the steps on which she was seated. The cat did not move. Instead she purred very faintly. It was a sound that was scarcely a sound. It was a barely distinguishable vibration in the pale afternoon air. Her amber eyes did not blink but they narrowed slightly — anticipating his touch which followed at once. His fingers met the soft crown of her head and moved down over the bony furred ridge of her back: under his fingers he felt the faint, faint quiver of her body as she purred. She raised her head slightly to gaze up at him. It was a feminine gesture: the gesture of a woman who glances up at her lover's face as he embraces her, a rapt, sightless glance, undeliberate as the act of breathing.

"Do you like cats?"

The voice was directly above him. It belonged to a large blonde woman in a gingham dress.

Lucio flushed guiltily and the woman laughed.

"Her name is Nitchevo," said the woman.

He repeated the name haltingly.

"Yes, it's peculiar," she said. "One of our roomers give her that name Nitchevo. He was a Russian or something. Stayed here before he took sick. He found that cat in an alley and brought her home an' fed her an' took care of her an' let her sleep in his bed, an' now we can't get rid of th' dog-gone thing. Twice already today I thrown cold water on her and still she sits! — I guess she's waitin' for him to come back home. But he won't, though. I was havin' a conversation the other day with some boys he used to work with down at the plant. It's too bad now. They tell me he's right on the verge of kickin' the bucket out west where he went for his lungs when he started to spit up blood. — Tough luck is what I call it. — He wasn't a bad sort of a fellow as them Polacks go."

Her voice trailed off and she turned away, smiling vaguely, as if to go back inside.

"Do you keep boarders?" he asked.

"No," said the woman. "Everybody along here does but us. My husband is not a very well man anymore. Got hurt in an accident down at the plant and now he's not

good for nothing except being tooken care of. So me —"
she sighed, "I got to work out at that bakery down on
James Street."

She laughed and held up her palms, the sweating lines
of which were traced with a chalky whiteness.

"That's how I got all this flour. My next-door-neigh-
bor, Mizz Jacoby, tells me I smell like a fresh loaf of
bread. Well — I don't have time to keep boarders, all I
can keep is roomers. I got rooms I could show you — if
you would be interested."

She paused in good-humored reflection — stroked her
hips and allowed her gaze to slide off on a gentle excursion among the barren tree-tops.

"As a matter of fack," she continued, "I guess I could
show you that room the Russian vacated. If you ain't
superstitious about occupying the room that a man took
sick in as bad as that. They say that it ain't contagious
but I don't know."

She turned and went into the house and Lucio followed.

She showed him the room that the Russian had lately
moved out of. It had two windows, one that faced the
brick wall of a laundry that smelled of naptha, another
that opened upon a narrow back-yard where greenish-
blue cabbage heads were scattered about like static foun-
tains of sea-water among the casual clumps of unweeded
grass.

As he looked out that back window and the woman
stood behind him, breathing warmly upon the nape of
his neck and smelling of flour, he saw Nitchevo, the

cat, picking her way with slow grace among the giant cabbage-heads.

"Nitchevo," remarked the woman.

"What does it mean?" he asked her.

"Oh, I don't know. I guess something crazy in Russian. — He told me but I forgotten."

"I'll take the room if I can do like the Russian and keep the cat here with me."

"Oh!" laughed the woman. "You want to do like the *Russian!*"

"Yes," said Lucio.

"Him an' me were pretty good friends," she told him. "He helped me out with things my husband ain't good for now that he's had that accident down at the plant."

"Yes? — Well, how about it?"

"Well —" she sat down on the bed. "I never take nobody in without talking a little. There's some things I like to be sure of before I make final arrangements. — You understand that."

"Oh, yes."

"For instance, I don't like fairies."

"What?"

"Fairies! — I had one once that used to go out on the street in a red silk scarf and bring men back to the room. — I don't like that."

"I wouldn't do that."

"Well, I just wanted to know. You looked kind of strange."

"I'm foreign."

"What kind of foreigner are you?"

"My folks were Sicilians."

"What?"

"An island near Italy."

"Oh. — I guess that's all right."

She looked at him — winked and grinned.

"Musso!" she said. "That's what I'll call you —
*Musso!*"

Ponderously coquettish, she rose from the bed and
poked him in the stomach with her thumb.

"Well — how about it?" he asked her.

"Okay. — Have you got a job yet?"

"Not yet."

"Go down to the plant and ask for Oliver Woodson.
Tell him Mizz Hutcheson sent yuh. — He'll give you a
job all right with my recommendation."

"Thank you — *thank* you!"

She grinned and chuckled and sighed and turned
slowly away. "My husband has got the war-news on the
radio all of the time. — It gives me a pain in the place
that I sit down on. — But a sick man's got to be humored.
— That's how it is."

But Lucio wasn't listening. He had turned back to the
window to look at the cat. She was still down there in the
yard, patiently waiting between two large cabbage-
heads to receive the verdict that settled her future existence. Oh, what a passion of longing there was in her
look. But dignity, too.

Quickly he moved past the woman and down the
front stairs.

"Where are you going?" she called.

"Out! In back! — For the cat!"

Lucio got a job at the plant through the man named Woodson. The work that he did was what he had always done, a thing that you did with your fingers without much thought. A chain clanked beneath you, you made some little adjustment, the chain moved on. But each time it moved beyond your place in the line it took a part of you with it. The energy in your fingers was drained out slowly. It was replaced by energy further back in your body. Then this was drained out also. When the day ended you were left feeling empty. What had gone out of you? Where had it gone to? *Why?* — You bought the evening papers the yelling boys poked toward you. Maybe here was a clue to all of these questions. Perhaps the latest edition would tell you what you lived for and why you labored. But no! The papers avoided that subject. Instead they announced the total amount of tonnage now lost at sea. The number of planes brought down in aerial combat. Cities captured, towns bombarded. —The facts were confusing, the paper fell out of your fingers, your head ached dully. . . .

Oh, my God, and when you got up in the morning, there was the sun in the same position you saw it the day before — beginning to rise from the graveyard back of the street, as though its nightly custodians were the fleshless dead — seen through the town's invariable smoke haze, it was a ruddy biscuit, round and red, when it might just as well have been square or shaped like a worm — anything might have been anything else and had as much meaning to it. . . .

The foreman seemed to dislike him, or maybe suspect him of something. Often he stopped directly behind Lucio's back and watched him working — stood there an unnecessarily long time and before he moved off always grunted a little and in a way that suggested any number of menacing possibilities.

Lucio thought to himself: I will not be able to keep this job very long.

He wrote his brother a letter. —This brother named Silva was serving a ten-year sentence in a Texas prison. He was Lucio's twin but their natures were not alike. Yet they were close to each other. Silva had been the rebel, a boy who loved music and whiskey, whose life was nocturnal as the life of a cat, a sleek young man he had been, with always the delicate scent of women about him. His clothes flung carelessly about the flat, which they had shared in the town further south, were faintly dusted with powder from women's bodies. Small trinklets tumbled out of his pockets, testimonials of intimacy with Gladys or Mabel or Ruth. When he awoke he always wound up the victrola and when he wanted to sleep, he switched the radio off. — Lucio rarely saw him either awake or asleep. They very seldom discussed their lives with each other but once Lucio found a revolver in his brother's coat-pocket. He left the revolver on the bed which they used at opposite hours — under it he placed a pencilled note. This is your death, said the note. When he came home the revolver had disappeared. In its place on the bed was a pair of workman's gloves that Lucio used at the foundry. Pinned to it was a note in Silva's irregu-

lar hand. Here is *yours,* said the note. — Shortly thereafter Silva had gone to Texas and there was arrested and
given a ten-year term on a holdup charge. Lucio started
the letters which now had gone on for eight years. Each
time he wrote he informed his brother of some purely
fanciful advancement in his career. He told him that he
had become a foreman and a stockholder in the corporation. That he belonged to a country-club and drove a
Cadillac car — that recently he had moved north to assume a much better position with several times as much
pay. These lies were further and further elaborated:
they began to comprise a sort of dream existence. His
face flushed while he wrote them — his hand shook so
that toward the end of the letter the writing would be
illegible almost. It was not that he wanted to arouse his
unfortunate brother's envy, it was not that at all. — But
he had loved the brother intensely and Silva had always
been so contemptuous of him in a kind sort of way. —
Silva apparently believed the news in the letters. How
well you are doing! he wrote. You could see he was
startled and proud — so that Lucio thought with dread
of the time when the truth must be known, when his
brother got out of the prison. . . .

Lucio's feeling that he could not long hold the job
became an obsession with him: a certain knowledge that
clung to his brain all the time. In the evenings, with
Nitchevo the cat, he could shut it partly away. Nitchevo's presence was a denial of all the many threatening
elements of chance. You could see that Nitchevo did not
take stock in chance. She believed that everything prog-

ressed according to a natural, predestined order and that there was nothing to be apprehensive about. All of her movements were slow and without agitation. They were accomplished with a consummate grace. Her amber eyes regarded each object with unblinking serenity. Even about her food she made no haste. Each evening Lucio brought home a pint of milk for her supper and breakfast: Nitchevo sat quietly waiting on her haunches while he poured it into the cracked saucer borrowed from the landlady and set it on the floor beside the bed. Then he lay down on the bed, expectantly watching, while Nitchevo came slowly forward to the pale blue saucer. She looked up at him once — slowly — with her unflickering yellow eyes before she started to eat, and then she gracefully lowered her small chin to the saucer's edge, the red satin tip of tongue protruded and the room was filled with the sweet, faint music of her gentle lapping. He watched her and as he watched her his mind smoothed out. The tight knots of anxiety loosened and were absorbed. The compressed and gaseous feeling inside his body was forgotten and his heart beat more quietly. He began to feel sleepy as he watched the cat — sleepy and entranced. Her form grew in size and the rest of the room dwindled and receded. It seemed to him, then, that they were of equal dimensions. He was a cat like Nitchevo — they lay side by side on the floor, lapping milk in the comfortable, secure warmth of a locked room beyond which no factories or foremen existed, nor large blonde landladies with hauntingly full-fleshed bosoms.

Nitchevo took a long time about drinking her milk. Often he was asleep before she had finished. He would awake later on and find her small warmth against him — he would sleepily raise his hand to caress her and he would feel the faint, faint vibration of the vertebral ridges along her back as she purred. She was getting fatter. Her sides filled out. — Of course there had been no spoken declaration of love between the two of them, but each understood that a contract existed between them to last their whole lives. Lucio talked to the cat in drowsy whispers — he never fabricated such stories as those that he wrote to his brother but merely denials of worries that plagued him most. He told her that he was not going to lose his job, that he would always be able to give her the saucer of milk night and morning and let her sleep on his bed; he told her that nothing disastrous was going to happen to them, that there was nothing to be afraid of between heaven and earth. Not even the sun, that rose newly-burnished each day from the heart of the cemetery, would break the enchantment which they had established between them.

One evening Lucio fell asleep with the light in his room still burning. The landlady, who was sleepless that night, saw it shining under the crack of his door and she came to the door and knocked and getting no response, she pushed it open. She found the strange little man asleep on the bed with the cat curled against his bare chest. His face was sharp and prematurely aged and his eyes, when they were open, made it look older still, but now they were closed, and his body was thin and white and under-developed like that of a spindly boy. He did not look like very much of a man, she observed. But she wanted to test his manhood. The Russian had also been thin, cadaverous almost, and always coughing as though an army of vandals were tearing him down from inside. Nevertheless, there had been a great fire in his nature which magnified him as a lover, made him assume almost a great physical stature. So she remembered the Russian who occupied that room before and she came to the side of the bed and threw the cat down to the floor and placed her hand on the sleeping little man's shoulder. Lucio woke and found her seated beside him, smiling, still smelling of the bed's warmth and faintly of flour. Her face was double in his unfocussed vision. Two large beaming moons that swam in the room's amber glow. Her hand on his shoulder burnt him, stung him painfully as the hide of a steaming horse had once stung his fingers when he touched it as a child. Her mouth was wet, the heat of her bosom engulfed him. The roses upon the wallpaper — how large they were! — And then they sank back into shadow. . . .

When the landlady had gone he went back to sleep again, scarcely aware of what had happened between them — except that now he felt more completely rested and quiet and the bed, it seemed to have risen to a great height over the dark, huddled roofs and bristling stacks of the factory town — and to be floating loose among stars that were not as chill as they looked, but warm with a human warmth that was scented with flour. . . .

THE life in the house grew sweet and familiar to him.

Sometimes when he entered the downstairs hall at fifteen after five on a wintry evening, he called out loudly and bravely, Heigho, Everybody, heigho! The blonde landlady moved out from the radio noise as though she was drugged, with a body stuffed full of honey-sweet popular songs — moons, roses, blue skies, rainbows after showers, cottages, sunsets, gardens, loves lasting forever! — She smiled with so much of it in her and touched her broad forehead and let her hand slide down her body, pressing herself here and there and enjoying the knowledge of so much sweet flesh on her and willing to share it. . . . Yes, yes, moons, lovers, roses — followed him up the hallstairs and into his bedroom and spilled themselves over the bed in a great, wild heap of "I love you!" —"Remember me always" and "Meet me tonight by the moonlight!" — the radio filled her up like a ten-gallon jug which the dark little man un-stoppered upstairs before supper.

But the work-a-day life in the plant was more and more strained. Lucio went at this work with a feverish haste, his anxiety coiling up tight whenever the foreman stopped at his place in the line. The grunt which he uttered, somewhat louder each time, was like a knife thrust into the center of Lucio's back: all his blood flowed out through the wound so that he scarcely had strength to remain on his feet. His hands went faster and faster until they lost their rhythm and the metal strips jammed and the machine cried out in a loud and furious voice, which ended abruptly the man's illusion as master.

"God damn!" said the foreman, "Why dontcha watch whatcha doin'? I'm tired a the way yuh bung up things all a time with yuh jittery fingers!"

He wrote to his brother that night that he had received another considerable boost in salary: he enclosed three dollars for candy and cigarettes and said that he was planning to engage another great lawyer to re-open Silva's case and take it, if necessary, to the United States Supreme Court.

"In the meantime," he ended, "sit tight! —There is nothing to worry about—absolutely."

This was the same type of statement he made every night to the cat.

But only a few days later there came a letter from the warden of the Texas prison, a man with the curious name of Mortimer J. Stallcup, returning the money and tersely announcing the convict brother, Silva, had recently been shot dead in an attempted jail-break.

Lucio showed this letter to his friend the cat. At first she seemed to observe it without much feeling. Then she became interested — she poked it with one white, tentative paw, mewed and set her teeth into a corner of the crisp paper. Lucio dropped it to the floor and she pushed it gently across the rug with her nose and her paws.

After a while he got up and poured out her milk which had grown rather warm in the steam-heated room. The radiators hissed. Her tongue lapped gently. —The roses on the wall-paper shimmered through tears that drained all the tension out of the little man's body.

Returning from the plant one evening that winter he

had a rather curious adventure. There was a place a few blocks from the plant called the Bright Spot Cafe. Out of it on this particular evening stumbled a man who looked like a plain street beggar. He caught at Lucio's sleeve and after a long, steady glance with eyes as enflamed as the cemetery-horizon before daybreak, he made a remarkable statement:

"Don't be afraid of these stinking sons-of-bitches. They grow like weeds and like stink-weeds are cut down. They run away from their conscience and can't be still for a minute. —Watch for the sun! — It comes up out of their graveyard every morning!"

The speech rambled on for some time in prophetic vein — when at last he let go of Lucio's arm, to which he clung for support, he headed back to the swinging door he emerged from. Just before going inside he made a final statement which struck home profoundly.

*"Do you know who I am?"* he shouted. *"I'm God Almighty!"*

"What?" said Lucio.

The old man nodded and grinned — waved in farewell and passed back into the brightly-lighted cafe.

Lucio knew that the old man was probably drunk and a liar but like most people he sometimes had the ability to believe what he wanted to believe in despite of all logic. And so there were nights that harsh, northern winter when he comforted himself and the cat with the recollection of the old man's statement. God was perhaps, he remembered, a resident of this strangely devitiated city whose grey-brown houses were like the dried skins of locusts. God was, like Lucio, a lonely and bewildered man Who felt that something was wrong but could not correct it, a man Who sensed the blundering sleep-walk of time and hostilities of chance and wanted to hide Himself from them in places of brilliance and warmth.

Nitchevo the cat did not need to be told that God had taken up his residence in the factory town. She had already discovered his presence twice: first in the Russian, then in Lucio. It is doubtful that she really distinguished between them. They both represented the same quality of infinite mercy. They made her life safe and pleasant. From the alley they had brought her to the house. The house was warm, the rugs and the pillows were soft. She rested in perfect content, a content which was not, like Lucio's, merely nocturnal but stayed with her all through the days as well as the nights—which was never broken. (If He the Creator did not order all things well, He conferred one inestimable benefit in the animal kingdom when He deprived all but man of the disquieting faculty of examining the future.) Nitchevo, being a cat, existed in only one sliding moment of time: that moment was good. It did not occur to the cat that convicts might be attempting escapes from Texas prisons and being shot down (which accident terminated escape through dream) that wardens were writing terse letters announcing such facts, that foremen grunted contemptuously when they stood behind men whose fingers trembled with fear of doing things badly. That wheels cried out and cracked the whip as the master. That men were blind who thought they saw things plainly, that God had been driven to drink — Nitchevo did not know that this curious accident of matter, the earth, was whirling dangerously fast and some day, unexpectedly, it would fly apart from its own excessive momentum and shatter itself into little bits of disaster.

Nitchevo purred under Lucio's fingers in absolute contradiction of all circumstances that threatened their common existence — and that was perhaps why Lucio loved her so much.

It was now mid-January and every morning the wind with a tireless impatience would grab at the smoke of the plant and thrust it south-east of the town where it hung in a restless bank above the grave-yard: the sun rose through it at seven o'clock in the morning, red as the eyeball of a drunken beggar, and stared accusingly till it sank again on the opposite side, across the turgid river: the river kept running away, polluted, ashamed, looking neither to the right nor to the left, but steadily running and running. The final week of the month the stock-holders came in town for a crucial meeting. Glittering black and rushing close to the earth as beetles on desperate errands, the limousines sped toward the plant: disgorged their corpulent contents at private doorways and waited uneasily, like a nest of roaches, in cinder-covered parkways back of the plant.

What was hatching inside the conference chambers no one who actually worked at the plant could tell. It took some time for the eggs to incubate: secret and black and laid in coagulate clusters, they ripened slowly.

This was the problem: there was a slump at the plant. The stockholders had to decide what action to take, whether to cheapen the product and make it available thus to a wider market or else cut down on production. The answer was obvious: they would cut down on production, preserving the margin of profit, and wait for the need of the people to make more demand. This was promptly arranged. The wheels got their orders and stopped: the workers were stopped by the wheels. One third of the plant shut down and the men were laid off: the black roach-nest dispersed from the cinder parkway: the problem was solved.

Lucio — yes — was among them.

There were sixty-eight of them given their notices that morning. There was no protest, there was no demonstration, no angry voices were lifted. It was almost as though these sixty-eight factory workers had known from the beginning that this was in store. Perhaps in the wombs of their mothers the veins that had fed them had sung in their ears this song: Thou shalt lose thy job, thou shalt be turned away from the wheels and the bread taken from thee!

It was a glittering wasteland, the town that morning. All week the snow had fallen, lightless and thick. But now the sun shone upon it. Each separate crystal was radiant and alive. The roofs were exclamatory. The steep, narrow streets were ruthlessly brilliant as arrows.

*Cold, cold, cold is the merciless blood of thy father!*

In Lucio two things competed. One was the need to find his companion the cat. The other and equal need

50

was that of his body to loosen its agonized tension, to fall, to let go, to be swept on like a river.

He managed to keep on walking as far as the Bright Spot Cafe.

There he was met by the man he had met once before, the beggarly stranger, the man who had called himself God.

Out of the lively, rotating glass door of this building the stranger emerged with an armful of empty beer-bottles the management had rejected because they were not purchased there.

"Like weeds," he repeated glumly, "like noxious weeds!"

He pointed south-east of the town with the arm not burdened with bottles.

"Watch for the sun. It comes from the cemetery."

His spittle gleamed in the terrible glare of the morning.

"I clench my fist and this is the fist of God."

Then he noticed the discharged worker before him.

"Where do you come from?" he asked.

"The plant," said Lucio faintly.

The angry glow in the blood-shot eyes waxed brighter.

"The plant, *the plant!*" groaned the stranger.

His small black shoe, bound up with adhesive tape and wads of paper, spattered the snow as it stamped.

He shook his fist in the bristling stacks' direction.

"Cupidity and stupidity!" he shouted. "That is the two-armed cross on which they have nailed me!"

An iron-loaded truck came by with a sloshing thunder.

The old man's face convulsed with rage as it passed.

"Lies, lies, lies, lies!" he shouted. "They've covered their bodies with lies and they won't stand washing! They want to be scabbed all over, they want no skin but the crust of their greediness on them! Okay, okay, let 'em have it! But let 'em have *more* and *more!* Maggots as well as lice! Yeah, pile th' friggin' dirt of their friggin' graveyard on 'em, shovel 'em under *deep* — till I can't *smell* 'em!"

THE sound of this malediction was drowned in another truck's thunder, but Lucio heard the man's words. He stopped on the walk beside him. The stranger's vehemence was so great he had dropped his bottles. Together they crouched to the walk and picked them up with the grave and voiceless preoccupation of children gathering flowers. When they were finished and he, the stranger, had spat out the phlegm that choked him, he caught hold of Lucio's arm and peered at him wildly.

"Where are you going?" he asked.

"Home," the little man told him, "I'm going home."

"Yes, go home," said the stranger. "Back to the bowels of earth. But not forever. The humble cannot be destroyed, they keep on going!"

"Going?" asked Lucio. "*Where?*"

"Where?" said the prophet, "*Where?* — I don't know *where!*" He began to sob — his sobbing shook him so that he dropped the bottles once more. And this time when Lucio crouched to assist in the gathering up, his strength went from him suddenly in a wave that swept far out and left him stranded, empty and flat and very nearly lifeless, upon the walk in the rapidly blackening snow outside the cafe.

"Drunk," said the burly policeman.

The man who had called himself God protested but he could do nothing.

The wagon was called and Lucio thrust inside it.

"Nitchevo, Nitchevo," was all he could say when they asked him where his home was. — So they bore him away.

For nearly an hour the man who called himself God remained on the corner outside of the Bright Spot Cafe. He appeared to be puzzled by something.

At last he shrugged and moved on down the street to the next beer-parlor.


WHAT is your name? What did your mother die of? Do you have dreams at night?

No, no, no, no. No name, no mother, no dreams. Please leave me alone.

He was a very bad patient. Refuses to co-operate, the doctors decided.

Finally after a week they turned him away.

He went directly back to the rooming-house. The door was unlocked. The hall was frosty and silent.

Where was the cat? Not there, he could tell without asking. If she had been there he would have been able to feel her breath in the stillness. There would have been something liquid and warm in the air like the womb of the mother remembered a long way off.

Mrs. Hutcheson heard him and came from the rear of the house where the radio blared a ceaseless popular dream.

"I heard that you'd been laid off," was all that she said.

It was easy to see that the Swanee and roses and moonlight had been turned off to meet a stricter occasion. Her amplitude now was hostile. It blocked his way.

He started to go upstairs but she blocked the staircase.

"The room has been taken," she told him.

"Oh."

"I can't afford to let my rooms be vacant."

"No."

"I got to be practical, don't I?"

"Yes."

"Everyone's got to be practical. That's how it is."

"I see. —Where is the cat?"

"The cat? —I turned her out Wednesday."

Now for the last time vehemence stirred inside him. Energy. Anger. Protest.

"No, no, no!" he shouted.

"Be still!" said the woman. "What do you think I am? The nerve of some people — expect me to play nursemaid to a sick alley-cat!"

"Sick?" said Lucio — he was suddenly quiet.

"Yes," said the woman.

"What was the matter with her?"

"How should I know? — She cried all night and created an awful disturbance. — I turned her out."

"Where did she go?"

The woman laughed harshly. "Where did she go! How on earth should I know where that dirty cat went! She might have gone to the devil for all I know!"

Her great bulk turned and she climbed back up the stairs. The door of Lucio's former room stood open. The woman entered. A male voice spoke her name and the door was closed.

Lucio went back out of the enemy's house.

Dimly, remotely, and without any definite feeling, he knew that the game was up. Yes, he could see behind him the whole of his time on earth. Mad pilgrimage of the flesh. Its twistings and turnings, its seemingly empty excursions. He saw how the lines, delusively parallel-seeming, had now converged and had made all forward motion impossible from now on.

He was not conscious of fear nor self-pity nor even regret anymore.

He walked to the corner and turned instinctively down.

Then there occurred once more and for the last time in his life a great and a merciful thing: an act of God.

At the entrance of an alley just beyond where he stood he saw abruptly the limping and oddly-misshapen figure of his lost companion. —The *cat!* Yes! Nitchevo!

He stood quite still and let his friend approach him. This she did, but with great difficulty. Their eyes were ropes that drew them slowly together in spite of the body's resistance. For she was hurt very badly, she could hardly move....

The consummation was gradual. Still it progressed.

And all of the time the eyes of the cat stayed on him.

Her amber eyes regarded him with their usual dignified, unquestioning devotion as though he had only returned from a few minutes' absence and not after days and days of hunger, calamity, cold.

Lucio reached down and gathered her into his arms. He observed now the cause of her limping. One of her legs had been crushed. It must have been for several days in that condition. It had festered and turned black and was very ill-smelling. Her body in his arms felt like a tiny bundle of bones and the sound that she made to greet him was less than a sound.

How had it happened, this injury? Nitchevo could not tell him. Neither could he tell her what had happened to him. He could not describe the foreman who watched and grunted, the calm superiority of doctors, nor the landlady, blond and dirty, in whom desire could be satisfied as well by one man as another.

Silence and physical closeness spoke for them both.

He knew she could not go on living. She knew it, too. Her eyes were tired and dark: eclipsed in them now was that small, sturdy flame which means a desire to go on and which is the secret of life's heroic survival. No. The eyes were eclipsed. They were full to the amber brims with all of the secrets and sorrows the world can answer our ceaseless questioning with. Loneliness — yes. Hunger. Bewilderment. Pain. All of these things were in them. They wanted no more. They wanted now to be closed on what they had gathered and not have to hold any more.

56

He carried her down the steep, cobbled street toward the river. It was an easy direction. The whole town slanted that way.

The air had grown dark, no longer containing the terrible brilliance of sunlight reflected on snow. The wind took the smoke up quickly and sent it scudding across low roofs in sheep-like surrender. There was cold in the air and a sooty gathering darkness. The wind whined a little as thin metal wires drawn taut.

High up on the bank, on the levee, a truck rumbled past. It was loaded with ingots of metal. Iron from the forge of the plant that was soaring away into darkness as the earth averted this side of its face from the stinging slap of the sun and gradually gave it the other.

Lucio spoke to the cat as the stream climbed about them.

"Soon," he whispered. "Soon, soon, very soon."

Only a single instant she struggled against him: clawed his shoulder and arm in a moment of doubt. *My God, My God, why hast Thou forsaken me?* Then the ecstacy passed and her faith returned, they went away with the river. Away from the town, away and away from the town, as the smoke, the wind took from the chimneys—

Completely away.

# THE POET

# THE POET

THE poet distilled his own liquor and had become so accomplished in this art that he could produce a fermented drink from almost any kind of organic matter. He carried it in a flask strapped about his waist, and whenever fatigue overtook him he would stop at some lonely point and raise the flask to his lips. Then the world would change color as a soap-bubble penetrated by a ray of light and a great vitality would surge and break as a limitless ocean through him. The usual superfluity of impressions would fall away so that his senses would combine in a single vast ray of perception which blinded him to lesser phenomena and experience as candles might be eclipsed in a chamber of glass exposed to a cloudless meridian of the sun.

His existence was one of benevolent anarchy, for no one of his time was more immune to the influence of states and organizations. In populated sections he might subsist as a scavenger on the refuse of others, but in the open country he lived as a ruminant beast on whatever green things were acceptable to his stomach.

A tall and angular man with eyes of turquoise and skin of clear amber, he had the cleanliness and beauty of sculpture. Such beauty is not allowed to pass unnoticed. He had never sought out any contact with people except the ideal one of audience and poet, but it sometimes happened that the sexual hunger of strangers would be visited on him. This would occur when bodily exhaustion had overtaken him after some great expansion of vision and when he had crept for refuge into an areaway. While he was resting there some anonymous passerby, who prowled the alleys at night, might happen to notice the poet and enter beside him with hotly exploring fingers and ravenous lips. In daylight the poet would waken to find his clothing torn open and sometimes not only a dampness of mouths on his flesh but painful bruises, and sometimes also a coin or a ring or some other gateful token thrust in a pocket or in the palm of his hand, but he would straighten his clothes and continue upon his way without any shame or resentment, and the briefly lingering dampness of such embraces would outlast his memory of them.

MERCIFULLY it so happened that scratching about for existence had grown to be automatic. It occupied none of

62

his thought and did not intrude on the inner life of the man. His poems were not written down, for his was a genius of speech. An earlier period of his life had been spent in a singular kind of evangelism. Then he had gone into places of public resort and delivered speeches of exhortation. Hardly a day had gone by without some violence being used upon him. He was often imprisoned and still more often was beaten. But gradually rage was purified out of his nature. He saw the childishness of it. Then he fell into silence for a time. He entered the places and looked about him and left them, addressing no one. For several years this retreat into silence continued. When it was broken, the character of his speech had changed entirely. The moral anger had given place to the telling of marvelous stories which he told in the open. His audience, then, was found among adolescents, boys and girls who were poised for that brief and hesitant spell between the coming of wisdom and its wilful rejection which is the condition on which the young are admitted to pockets of social states based on nothing pure in their natures. The poet had learned that his audience could only be found in this particular age-group. Now wherever he went he would gather about him the young and beautiful listeners to stories. He would pick them up at the entrances to schools and parks and playgrounds. His very appearance would magnetize the young people. Instinctively they would know him as a man who had dared to resist the will of the organizations which they would be forced to succumb to. Adults would judge him to be a worthless crank of some kind, but the young were drawn to him with a mysterious yearning and hung on his syllables as bees cluster on the inexhaustible chalice of a flower.

WHOEVER loves the young loves also the sea. It was therefore natural that the latter phase of the poet's life should be spent on the sea-coast. For ten months, now, he had lived on a tropical coast whose tremendous scape of open water and sky provided his stories with an ideal *mise-en-scène*. He had occupied a little driftwood shack. He could not remember if he had built it himself or found it already erected. It was situated at a point where the beach curved gently and smoothly inland and rose in a fanlike sweep of golden dunes. In a large iron drum, cast up from a wreck at sea, he had distilled his liquor of fiery potency and he kept this reservoir buried in sand behind his driftwood lodging.

Whenever he gave them a signal, his youthful audience would assemble about him and each time more would come and each time from villages which were further removed. For a long time, now, the poet had felt that his stories so far had been little more than preliminary exercises to some really great outpouring which might be more of a plastic than verbal creation. He felt that this culmination was now close at hand. The imminence grew in him with the warnings of fever. His body burned and thinned and his gold hair whitened. His heart had swollen. The arteries were distended. At times he would seem to be holding an incubus in his bosom, whose fierce little purplish knot of a head was butting against his ribs and whose limbs were kicking and squirming with convulsions. Now and again arterial blood would spurt from his mouth and nostrils. He noticed these warnings of death's unspeakable outrage encroaching upon him, but felt he had power enough to hold it in check until the event that he lived for had come to pass. It came that summer, late in the crazed month of August. The night preceding its coming the poet had wandered along the beach in a state of delirium in which he seemed to be making a steep ascent without any effort of breathlessness of climbing and at the height of this progress he could see below him as a picture puzzle with all its pieces fitted precisely together the whole of his time on earth. He noted triumphantly that the scattered instances had closed in a design and that the design could be closed into a vision. When morning came, it dropped him down the whole way, but he knew for what purpose. It was to call the children. A signal fire must be lit to summon the children. He started immediately to prepare it. But for the first time the inflammable stuff was difficult to gather. The fragments of dried wood seemed to be miles separated. He probed for them in the dunes and among the scrubby bushes until his knuckles were bleeding and the incubus in his breast had all but broken through the crumbling cage of his ribs. When finally there was enough to light the signal, a wind sprang up and he had to oppose the wind. He had to crouch over the flames till they blackened the skin of his chest and he had to embrace the fiery sticks with his arms to hold them together. Then all at once the opposition was over. The ocean took back the wind. The air was motionless and the ocean appeared to be struck like a statue in a blaze of calm, and now the pillar of smoke rose thin and straight as a tree without any branches. The poet withdrew from the point of fiendish trial, dragging himself on hands and knees to the merciful restoration held in the drum. A single taste of it lifted him to his feet. Once more and for the last time, the limitless ocean surged and broke in his veins, that ocean of scarlet the butterfly boat rocks on, which is being alive.

The pillar of smoke soon caught the children's attention. With faces barely washed for the early morning, they rose like birds from the villages to surge up the hillsides and tumble crazily down them, past the fenced in fields where their parents labored the soil, past doorways where old women crouched in dull astonishment at their windy passage, past everything stationary, incensed as they were by the demon of rushing forward, responding as only the ones of their age could respond to anything thin as smoke but promising vision.

A LONG way off the poet could hear their cries and knew they were coming. He rose from beside the drum and walked erect and powerful to the end of the beach where the children would appear. With clothing cast off along the course of their journey and nude bodies shining with wetness, the children swept over the last separating dune and enveloped the waiting figure of the poet.

In front of his driftwood lodging he brought them

66

to rest. There he stood in their midst and began his story. The scaffolding of the heavens remained very high and he proceeded to build a stairs for the children. They let their playthings go. The puppets of painted wreckage which he had carved for the children fell from their clasp as they began to take part in the narrative's action. They chased each other among the scarves of foam. Their leaps were prodigious, their shouts were everlasting, and always he called them back for another lesson, stretching his wasted arms like the cross-bars of a ship on a drunken ocean. He compelled them to understand the rapture of vision and how it could let a man break out of his body. Before the slanting wall of the driftwood house, his eyes shot arrows of pale blue lightning at them, he leaned and gestured and imitated the ocean. A huge blue rocking-horse seemed to be loose among them whose plumes were smoky blue ones the sky could not hold and so let grandly go of.

The story continued till dusk, and at that time the children's parents came for them. The men of the villages had become suspicious of the poet. They now surrounded his lodging and called him out. The poet came out and stood exhausted among them, peering almost blindly into their faces, now that the poetry had forsaken his body and left him old and wasted and shrunken grey. Without any explanation they told him to leave. The poet nodded agreement to their command, and frowned with sorrow, seeing the children far away on the beach and moving further among the shepherding mothers.

When all the dispersing crowd had gone from sight,

the poet returned to his house. He wrapped in a piece of sail-cloth his small collection of things, mementoes of distances walked along the ocean. He said goodbye to the ocean. He waved to it gravely with one of his hands that were like the arrowy skeletons of birds. He turned back inland after his ten months' stay on the shore of the ocean. When he had climbed with an effort that took his breath to the highest dune and had turned and looked behind him where his residence of driftwood appeared even smaller than it actually was as it huddled in growing night and in emptiness now at the edge of the plunging surf, he felt that finally all of his gold was spent and that what remained was only the clink of copper. Suddenly he resisted the thought of exile. He was bound to this place by more than ten months' custom. This was the place where he had finally told his greatest story, and if he would be remembered at all, it could only be here, by the children of this coastal region.

Staggering with exhaustion the poet retraced his steps. Still for a moment as he approached the ocean his brain could hold it. His vision still contained it. Then it rocked and split and the dark showed through it, tremendous and rushing toward him. He fell on the beach. His body remained at that spot for a long, long time. The sun and the sand and the water washed it continually and swept away all but the bones and the stiff white garments.

The children, scattering further than usual from their homes without the signal to draw them, happened at dusk on the skeleton of the poet. They had grown older but had not yet discarded their tender feelings. They circled about the skeleton of the poet, bewildered and sorrowful, aware of a loss they could not express to each other. One of them finally went to the great iron drum containing the poet's liquor. Having once seen the poet drink of it, he cupped his palm in the liquor and drank a portion. The others followed suit. It coursed as flame through their bodies and made them reel. They became very drunk and suddenly, of a single accord, they lay in the sand beside the huge iron drum and back of the driftwood shack, and thrust and plunged their bodies against each other.

Not far off shore two vessels engaged in battle. One of them was sunk, and as night fell, the bodies of drowned sailors washed onto the beach. The children, by that time exhausted, wandered along the beach and gazed at the bodies which were beginning already to wear the look of corruption. Alone among them the skeleton of the poet appeared immune to decay. And for the last time of all, for now they were old enough to be conscripted into the service of states and organizations, the children remotely sensed the presence of something outside the province of matter. Then they turned homewards. The wind blew about them odors of smoke and death as they returned to their villages, never again to rise from them as swallows when distant smoke announced to them, Here is vision!

CHRONICLE OF
A DEMISE

# CHRONICLE

# OF A DEMISE

The many letters which have come into my hands from provincial members of the Order requesting some information about our Saint's disappearance were left unanswered till now because among us at the Center some hope still persisted that we would be given a sign on which we could premise some faith in her transfiguration. That hope having lately been formally abandoned, there seems no longer to be any valid excuse for further withholding the facts set down hereunder.

Our Saint's admired exaltation, during the swift last summer of her life, the two months spent on a cot on the roof of her cousin's East Side apartment building, was due not so much to any profound resurgence of faith in the Order as it was to the coffee drunk black without sugar, two or three times a day on an empty stomach. This coffee was all that the Saint was willing to take from her cousin's table and this she only accepted because we had been assured that if she did not accept it, it would be poured down the kitchen drain.

The coffee was brought up to her not by the cousin himself but by his orphan nephew, a child of ten who was crippled and had some difficulty in climbing the stairs. On one occasion the crippled child stumbled as he was approaching the Saint with the pot of coffee and a small amount of the coffee was splashed on her forehead. Now I was a witness to this slight misadventure from which a rumor derived that the cousin's party had plotted to blind the Saint, and while I am not an apologist for the cousin's behavior, I consider it my duty to report that a bit of loose tar-paper on the roof and not any plot downstairs was responsible for the spilling of the coffee.

The coffee was always brought up in the battered aluminum percolator that it was prepared in. The Saint drank it from the percolator's spout, supporting herself on her elbows and looking out over the roof-tops toward the East River, where she believed she would see the ship returning if it returned that summer.

Under the cot was the scarlet heart-shaped box, once a container of Valentine's Day candies, in which were kept the articles of our faith. There appears no longer to be the slightest reason for holding back knowledge of how these things were collected. They were collected at random, in subway stations and under the seats of trains, in gutters and alleys of many different towns, even by theft from persons whose homes she visited while the Saint and myself were engaged in the membership drive.

The charge which was made by some members of the Left that the Saint had begun to entertain doubts in regard to the articles is based on the entrance for August first in my journal. Upon that date I had come to see her about the nomination of something that Agatha Doyle had placed in the "Possible Box." This article was a piece of purple tinfoil which Agatha had picked up on Father Duffy's Square. The Saint looked it over but seemed to be unimpressed. I put the article back in the "Possible Box." There was an interval of silence between us, and then the Saint, who had raised herself on her elbows to look at the article Agatha had proposed, dropped suddenly back on her pillow and made the remark which those on the Left construed as a disavowal.

The articles in the box are destructible matter.

That was all that she said, and it was said in a tone of no particular bitterness. It was somewhat unexpected, however, and I turned my face to the chimney in order to hide a momentary embarrassment while I transcribed the statement. The Saint reached out and took hold of my tablet and pencil and under the statement which I had just copied down , she wrote this highly significant addition.

*Matter is not what matters!* And then she smilingly handed back the journal.

I am sure you must see how far this actually was from

a disavowal. The fact it was so misconstrued is evidence of the extremes to which the Left was now carried in its determined effort to create a schism.

By the close of July the apostasy of the Saint's cousin had grown too apparent for anyone to ignore. His dwindling attendance had now fallen off to the point that he ceased to appear at the Saturday rearrangements. Once when a thunderstorm came from across the East River and made it advisable to take the collection downstairs, as the iron cot itself appeared to be in some danger of blowing away, the Cousin refused to have the articles placed in his apartment. He claimed that his wife had developed a strong nervous dread of the things in the box and that having them near her was likely to give her convulsions. The child with his leg in a brace delivered this message to us just as we were grouping about the box, preparatory to taking it downstairs. The Saint, supported on one side by Agatha Doyle and by myself on the other, was having a manifestation and seemed not to catch a single word of the message. The child, as he read it aloud from the typewritten sheet of coarse manila paper, was rubbing a bruise on his forearm, a purplish discoloration, which led me to feel that the mission had been forced upon him. The attitude of the child is not important, but extremists of both parties have attributed to him a sort of precocious Machiavellianism which fairness compels me to say was not borne out by anything I observed. He was innocent of design as a carrier-pigeon.

The child had already slipped back down the stairs before any of us who were attending the Saint had time to absorb the import of the message. Agatha Doyle let go of the Saint's right arm. The Saint bounded up like a paper kite on a string. I shouted, Agatha, what on earth are you doing? It took three others beside myself and Miss Doyle to haul the Saint back down. Of course by this time the manifestation had passed. She seemed to be stunned and we thought it best not to mention our reason for not removing the box from the roof. The storm had already passed over, at least the worst of it had. Agatha Doyle was securing the Saint to the cot with the belt of her dress, when, not five minutes after he gave us the message, the child reappeared and was bearing the percolator. I noted he had a second bruise on his arm, the same arm, but lower, close to the wrist and his eyes were inflamed as if the child had been weeping. He thrust the coffee-pot toward the recumbent Saint. Agatha took it first. She gave me a startled glance and passed it to me. I looked in the percolator and found it was empty. It had been thoroughly scoured. Not even an odor of coffee remained about it.

To all of us on the Right, and even to most of the so-called Liberal group, it was plainly evident that things could not go on as they had been going and that some sort of culmination was close at hand.

It came in the last week of August.

A record number of seven new articles had been placed in the Possible Box the night before, and a meeting had been called to consider the sanctification of a wad of Spearmint gum that Hannibal Weems had picked up on the steps of an escalator in Gimbel's department store the previous Tuesday. The rites of induction had been already concluded. The Saint, supported on one hand by Doster Parker and on the other by me, was delivering such an enraptured incantation that she appeared unaware of her cousin's tardy arrival on the roof. He had come out on the roof in ceremonial dress, complete with the one and rather shocking exception of worn canvas sneakers which had an offensive odor. He leaned against the chimney, looking on sullenly as the sanctified articles were installed in the Box. The seven new articles had been placed at the bottom. This was, of course, an arbitrary disposal. Under more usual circumstances, degrees of sanctity would have been determined and the articles put in strictly graded positions. This would have called for a twenty-four hour session which at the time not even the indefatigable Mr. Parker was in a condition to undertake without recess. All but four or five of us had gone downstairs to partake of a buffet supper, prepared and served by girls of the Junior Committee. A few of the party in power remained on the roof, near the Saint who had fallen silent and seemed to be exhausted. The party of Opposition was all withdrawn from the roof except for the Cousin. The Cousin began to mutter. He circled about the chimney several times, in widening orbits which bore him continually closer to the cot.

It was darkening in the East. On the other side of the river the great power-plant was already lighted up for the summer evening.

The Cousin at last spoke out, addressing the Saint.

I know what has happened, he said. The expedition

has returned and you are stalling for time because it came back empty-handed!

At this remark the Misses Doyle and La Mantia scrambled away from the cot like a pair of frightened hens and rushed pell-mell down the stairs. The Saint and her cousin and I were all that remained on the roof.

To my astonishment, then, the Saint replied, Yes, the expedition returned last week empty-handed.

What are your plans? asked the Cousin.

The Saint replied that the ship had already sailed on another voyage.

Secretly? asked the Cousin.

Of course, said the Saint.

The Cousin appeared to receive this answer calmly. Then all at once his arm shot out and grabbed hold of the box. It will have to end now! he shouted.

He flung the box with all his force from the roof.

There was a brief confusion.

The Saint drew open her gown and opened her chest. Her heart divided as leaves of thin tissue paper. The leaves blew out, they blew in the face of the Cousin who sputtered and coughed as though he had sniffed red pepper. I made an attempt to hold the leaves from dispersion. I caught a few of them and thrust the few I had caught back into the cleft of her bosom. But it was too late. The clock-spring was making a little rasping noise. Then this stopped, too. Her two clenched hands came open. Her eyeballs, hard and beautifully blue as marbles, sprung straight out on their glittering coiled attachments.

Let her go, said the Cousin.

We both released the limbs we were holding down. A fine cool spray was dashed back into our faces as all her tissues divided and lifted away. In half a minute she had gone altogether. The Cousin said nothing but stared at the empty cot. His wife could now be heard at the foot of the stairs calling him down to supper. He went without speaking and as there was obviously nothing more to be done, I followed him down from the roof, picked up my hat and silently left the building.

This is all that I have to report of the matter.

Now as for instructions, I really have none to give you. The Center has now disbanded and ceased to exist as an organizational unit. The future course of individual members is now a matter of individual choice. As for myself, I am intending to travel, but where I shall go and the purpose of my going are matters I feel at liberty not to divulge.

# DESIRE AND THE
# BLACK MASSEUR

# DESIRE AND THE

# BLACK MASSEUR

**F**ROM his very beginning this person, Anthony Burns, had betrayed an instinct for being included in things that swallowed him up. In his family there had been fifteen children and he the one given least notice, and when he went to work, after graduating from high school in the largest class on the records of that institution, he secured his job in the largest wholesale company of the city. Everything absorbed him and swallowed him up, and still he did not feel secure. He felt more secure at the movies than anywhere else. He loved to sit in the back rows of the movies where the darkness absorbed him gently so that he was like a particle of food dissolving in a big hot mouth. The cinema licked at his mind with a tender, flickering tongue that all but lulled him to sleep. Yes, a big motherly Nannie of a dog could not have licked him better or given him sweeter repose than the cinema did when he went there after work. His mouth would fall open at the movies and saliva would accumulate in it and dribble out the sides of it and all his being would relax so utterly that all the prickles and tightenings of a whole day's anxiety would be lifted away. He didn't follow the story on the screen but watched the figures. What they said or did was immaterial to him, he cared about only the figures who warmed him as if they were cuddled right next to him in the dark picture house and he loved every one of them but the ones with shrill voices.

The timidest kind of a person was Anthony Burns, always scuttling from one kind of protection to another but none of them ever being durable enough to suit him.

Now at the age of thirty, by virtue of so much protection, he still had in his face and body the unformed look of a child and he moved like a child in the presence of critical elders. In every move of his body and every inflection of speech and cast of expression there was a timid apology going out to the world for the little space that he had been somehow elected to occupy in it. His was not an inquiring type of mind. He only learned what he was required to learn and about himself he learned nothing. He had no idea of what his real desires were. Desire is something that is made to occupy a larger space than that which is afforded by the individual being, and this was especially true in the case of Anthony Burns. His desires, or rather his basic desire, was so much too big for him that it swallowed him up as a coat that should have been cut into ten smaller sizes, or rather there should have been that much more of Burns to make it fit him.

For the sins of the world are really only its partialities, its incompletions, and these are what sufferings must atone for. A wall that has been omitted from a house because the stones were exhausted, a room in a house left unfurnished because the householder's funds were not sufficient — these sorts of incompletions are usually covered up or glossed over by some kind of make-shift arrangement. The nature of man is full of such make-shift arrangements, devised by himself to cover his incompletion. He feels a part of himself to be like a missing wall or a room left unfurnished and he tries as well as he can to make up for it. The use of imagination, resorting to dreams or the loftier purpose of art, is a mask he devises to cover his incompletion. Or violence such as a war, between two men or among a number of nations, is also a blind and senseless compensation for that which is not yet formed in human nature. Then there is still another compensation. This one is found in the principle of atonement, the surrender of self to violent treatment by others with the idea of thereby clearing one's self of his guilt. This last way was the one that Anthony Burns unconsciously had elected.

Now at the age of thirty he was about to discover the instrument of his atonement. Like all other happenings in his life, it came about without intention or effort.

One afternoon, which was a Saturday afternoon in

85

November, he went from his work in the huge wholesale corporation to a place with a red neon sign that said
"Turkish Baths and Massage." He had been suffering
lately from a vague sort of ache near the base of his spine
and somebody else employed at the wholesale corporation had told him that he would be relieved by massage.
You would suppose that the mere suggestion of such a
thing would frighten him out of his wits, but when
desire lives constantly with fear, and no partition between them, desire must become very tricky; it has to
become as sly as the adversary, and this was one of those
times when desire outwitted the enemy under the roof.
At the very mention of the word "massage," the desire
woke up and exuded a sort of anesthetizing vapor all
through Burns' nerves, catching fear off guard and al-
lowing Burns to slip by it. Almost without knowing that
he was really going, he went to the baths that Saturday
afternoon.

The baths were situated in the basement of a hotel,
right at the center of the keyed-up mercantile nerves of
the downtown section, and yet the baths were a tiny
world of their own. Secrecy was the atmosphere of the
place and seemed to be its purpose. The entrance door
had an oval of milky glass through which you could
only detect a glimmer of light. And even when a patron
had been admitted, he found himself standing in laby-
rinths of partitions, of corridors and cubicles curtained
off from each other, of chambers with opaque doors and
milky globes over lights and sheathings of vapor. Everywhere were agencies of concealment. The bodies of

86

patrons, divested of their clothing, were swathed in billowing tent-like sheets of white fabric. They trailed barefooted along the moist white tiles, as white and noiseless as ghosts except for their breathing, and their faces all wore a nearly vacant expression. They drifted as if they had no thought to conduct them.

But now and again, across the central hallway, would step a masseur. The masseurs were Negroes. They seemed very dark and positive against the loose white hangings of the baths. They wore no sheets, they had on loose cotton drawers, and they moved about with force and resolution. They alone seemed to have an authority here. Their voices rang out boldly, never whispering in the sort of apologetic way that the patrons had in asking directions of them. This was their own rightful province, and they swept the white hangings aside with great black palms that you felt might just as easily have seized bolts of lightning and thrown them back at the clouds.

Anthony Burns stood more uncertainly than most near the entrance of the bath-house. Once he had gotten through the milky-paned door his fate was decided and no more action or will on his part was called for. He paid two-fifty, which was the price of a bath and massage, and from that moment forward had only to follow directions and submit to care. Within a few moments a Negro masseur came to Burns and propelled him onward and then around a corner where he was led into one of the curtained-compartments.

Take off your clothes, said the Negro.

87

The Negro had already sensed an unusual something about his latest patron and so he did not go out of the canvas-draped cubicle but remained leaning against a wall while Burns obeyed and undressed. The white man turned his face to the wall away from the Negro and fumbled awkwardly with his dark winter clothes. It took him a long time to get the clothes off his body, not because he wilfully lingered about it but because of a dream-like state in which he was deeply falling. A far-away feeling engulfed him and his hands and fingers did not seem to be his own, they were numb and hot as if they were caught in the clasp of someone standing be-hind him, manipulating their motions. But at last he stood naked, and when he turned slowly about to face the Negro masseur, the black giant's eyes appeared not to see him at all and yet they had a glitter not present before, a liquid brightness suggesting bits of wet coal.

Put this on, he directed and held out to Burns a white sheet.

Gratefully the little man enveloped himself in the enormous coarse fabric and, holding it delicately up from his small-boned, womanish feet, he followed the Negro masseur through another corridor of rustling white curtains to the entrance of an opaque glass enclo-sure which was the steam-room. There his conductor left him. The blank walls heaved and sighed as steam issued from them. It swirled about Burns' naked figure, en-veloping him in a heat and moisture such as the inside of a tremendous mouth, to be drugged and all but dis-solved in this burning white vapor which hissed out of unseen walls.

88

After a time the black masseur returned. With a mumbled command, he led the trembling Burns back into the cubicle where he had left his clothes. A bare white table had been wheeled into the chamber during Burns' absence.

Lie on this, said the Negro.

Burns obeyed. The black masseur poured alcohol on Burns' body, first on his chest and then on his belly and thighs. It ran all over him, biting at him like insects. He gasped a little and crossed his legs over the wild complaint of his groin. Then without any warning the Negro raised up his black palm and brought it down with a terrific whack on the middle of Burns' soft belly. The little man's breath flew out of his mouth in a gasp and for two or three moments he couldn't inhale another.

Immediately after the passing of the first shock, a feeling of pleasure went through him. It swept as a liquid from either end of his body and into the tingling hollow of his groin. He dared not look, but he knew what the Negro must see. The black giant was grinning.

I hope I didn't hit you too hard, he murmured.

No, said Burns.

Turn over, said the Negro.

Burns tried vainly to move but the luxurious tiredness made him unable to. The Negro laughed and gripped the small of his waist and flopped him over as easily as he might have turned a pillow. Then he began to belabor his shoulders and buttocks with blows that increased in violence, and as the violence and the pain increased, the little man grew more and more fiercely hot with his first true satisfaction, until all at once a knot came loose in his loins and released a warm flow.

So by surprise is a man's desire discovered, and once discovered, the only need is surrender, to take what comes and ask no questions about it: and this was something that Burns was expressly made for.

Time and again the white-collar clerk went back to the Negro masseur. The knowledge grew quickly between them of what Burns wanted, that he was in search of atonement, and the black masseur was the natural instrument of it. He hated white-skinned bodies because they abused his pride. He loved to have their white skin prone beneath him, to bring his fist or the palm of his hand down hard on its passive surface. He had barely been able to hold this love in restraint, to control the wish that he felt to pound more fiercely and use the full of his power. But now at long last the suitable person had entered his orbit of passion. In the white-collar clerk he had located all that he longed for.

Those times when the black giant relaxed, when he sat at the rear of the baths and smoked cigarettes or devoured a bar of candy, the image of Burns would loom before his mind, a nude white body with angry red marks on it. The bar of chocolate would stop just short of his lips and the lips would slacken into a dreamy smile. The giant loved Burns, and Burns adored the giant.

Burns had become absent-minded about his work. Right in the middle of typing a factory order, he would lean back at his desk and the giant would swim in the atmosphere before him. Then he would smile and his work-stiffened fingers would loosen and flop on the desk. Sometimes the boss would stop near him and call his name crossly. Burns! Burns! What are you dreaming about?

Throughout the winter the violence of the massage increased by fairly reasonable degrees, but when March came it was suddenly stepped up.

Burns left the baths one day with two broken ribs.

Every morning he hobbled to work more slowly and painfully but the state of his body could still be explained by saying he had rheumatism.

One day his boss asked him what he was doing for it. He told his boss that he was taking massage.

It don't seem to do you any good, said the boss.

Oh, yes, said Burns, I am showing lots of improvement!

That evening came his last visit to the baths.

His right leg was fractured. The blow which had broken the limb was so terrific that Burns had been unable to stifle an outcry. The manager of the bath establishment heard it and came into the compartment.

Burns was vomiting over the edge of the table.

Christ, said the manager, what's been going on here?

The black giant shrugged.

He asked me to hit him harder.

The manager looked over Burns and discovered his many bruises.

What do you think this is? A jungle? he asked the masseur.

Again the black giant shrugged.

Get the hell out of my place! the manager shouted. Take this perverted little monster with you, and neither of you had better show up here again!

The black giant tenderly lifted his drowsy partner and bore him away to a room in the town's Negro section.

There for a week the passion between them continued.

This interval was toward the end of the Lenten season. Across from the room where Burns and the Negro were staying there was a church whose open windows spilled out the mounting exhortations of a preacher. Each afternoon the fiery poem of death on the cross was repeated. The preacher was not fully conscious of what he wanted nor were the listeners, groaning and writhing before him. All of them were involved in a massive atonement.

Now and again some manifestation occurred, a woman stood up to expose a wound in her breast. Another had slashed an artery at her wrist.

Suffer, suffer, suffer! the preacher shouted. Our Lord was nailed on a cross for the sins of the world! They led him above the town to the place of the skull, they moistened his lips with vinegar on a sponge, they drove five nails through his body, and He was The Rose of the World as He bled on the cross!

The congregation could not remain in the building but tumbled out on the street in a crazed procession with clothes torn open.

The sins of the world are all forgiven! they shouted.

ALL during this celebration of human atonement, the Negro masseur was completing his purpose with Burns.

All the windows were open in the death-chamber.

The curtains blew out like thirsty little white tongues to lick at the street which seemed to reek with an overpowering honey. A house had caught fire on the block in back of the church. The walls collapsed and the cinders floated about in the gold atmosphere. The scarlet engines, the ladders and powerful hoses were useless against the purity of the flame.

The Negro masseur leaned over his still breathing victim.

Burns was whispering something.

The black giant nodded.

You know what you have to do now? the victim asked him. The black giant nodded.

He picked up the body, which barely held together, and placed it gently on a clean-swept table.

The giant began to devour the body of Burns.

It took him twenty-four hours to eat the splintered bones clean.

When he had finished, the sky was serenely blue, the passionate services at the church were finished, the ashes had settled, the scarlet engines had gone and the reek of honey was blown from the atmosphere.

Quiet had returned and there was an air of completion.

Those bare white bones, left over from Burns' atonement, were placed in a sack and borne to the end of a car-line.

There the masseur walked out on a lonely pier and dropped his burden under the lake's quiet surface.

As the giant turned homeward, he mused on his satisfaction.

Yes, it is perfect, he thought, it is now completed!

Then in the sack, in which he had carried the bones, he dropped his belongings, a neat blue suit to conceal his dangerous body, some buttons of pearl and a picture of Anthony Burns as a child of seven.

He moved to another city, obtained employment once more as an expert masseur. And there in a white-curtained place, serenely conscious of fate bringing toward him another, to suffer atonement as it had been suffered by Burns, he stood impassively waiting inside a milky white door for the next to arrive.

And meantime, slowly, with barely a thought of so doing, the earth's whole population twisted and writhed beneath the manipulation of night's black fingers and the white ones of day with skeletons splintered and flesh reduced to pulp, as out of this unlikely problem, the answer, perfection, was slowly evolved through torture.

# PORTRAIT OF
# A GIRL IN GLASS

# PORTRAIT OF A

# GIRL IN GLASS

W<small>E</small> lived in a third floor apartment on Maple
Street in Saint Louis, on a block which also contained
the Ever-ready Garage, a Chinese laundry, and a bookie
shop disguised as a cigar store.

Mine was an anomalous character, one that appeared
to be slated for radical change or disaster, for I was a
poet who had a job in a warehouse. As for my sister
Laura, she could be classified even less readily than I.
She made no positive motion toward the world but stood
at the edge of the water, so to speak, with feet that anti-
cipated too much cold to move. She'd never have budged
an inch, I'm pretty sure, if my mother who was a rela-
tively aggressive sort of woman had not shoved her

roughly forward, when Laura was twenty years old, by enrolling her as a student in a nearby business college. Out of her "magazine money" (she sold subscriptions to women's magazines), Mother had paid my sister's tuition for a term of six months. It did not work out. Laura tried to memorize the typewriter keyboard, she had a chart at home, she used to sit silently in front of it for hours, staring at it while she cleaned and polished her infinite number of little glass ornaments. She did this every evening after dinner. Mother would caution me to be very quiet. "Sister is looking at her typewriter chart!" I felt somehow that it would do her no good, and I was right. She would seem to know the positions of the keys until the weekly speed-drill got under way, and then they would fly from her mind like a bunch of startled birds.

At last she couldn't bring herself to enter the school any more. She kept this failure a secret for a while. She left the house each morning as before and spent six hours walking around the park. This was in February, and all the walking out-doors regardless of weather brought on influenza. She was in bed for a couple of weeks with a curiously happy little smile on her face. Of course Mother phoned the business college to let them know she was ill. Whoever was talking on the other end of the line had some trouble, it seems, in remembering who Laura was, which annoyed my mother and she spoke up pretty sharply. "Laura has been attending that school of yours for two months, you certainly ought to recognize her name!" Then came the stunning disclosure. The person sharply retorted, after a moment or two, that now she *did* remember the Wingfield girl, and that she had not been at the business college *once* in about a month. Mother's voice became strident. Another person was brought to the phone to verify the statement of the first. Mother hung up and went to Laura's bedroom where she lay with a tense and frightened look in place of the faint little smile. Yes, admitted my sister, what they said was true. "I couldn't go any longer, it scared me too much, it made me sick at the stomach!"

After this fiasco, my sister stayed at home and kept in her bedroom mostly. This was a narrow room that had two windows on a dusky areaway between two wings of the building. We called this areaway Death Valley for a reason that seems worth telling. There were a great many alley-cats in the neighborhood and one particularly vicious dirty white Chow who stalked them continually. In the open or on the fire-escapes they could usually elude him but now and again he cleverly contrived to run some youngster among them into the cul-de-sac of this narrow areaway at the far end of which, directly beneath my sister's bedroom windows, they made the blinding discovery that what had appeared to be an avenue of escape was really a locked arena, a gloomy vault of concrete and brick with walls too high for any cat to spring, in which they must suddenly turn to spit at their death until it was hurled upon them. Hardly a week went by without a repetition of this violent drama. The areaway had grown to be hateful to Laura because she could not look out on it without recalling the screams and the snarls of killing. She kept the shades drawn down, and as Mother would not permit the use of electric current except when needed, her days were spent almost in perpetual twilight. There were three pieces of dingy ivory furniture in the room, a bed, a bureau, a chair. Over the bed was a remarkably bad religious painting, a very effeminate head of Christ with teardrops visible just below the eyes. The charm of the room was produced by my sister's collection of glass. She loved colored glass and had covered the walls with shelves of little glass articles, all of them light and delicate in color. These she washed and polished with endless care. When you entered the room there was always this soft, transparent radiance in it which came from the glass absorbing whatever faint light came through the shades on Death Valley. I have no idea how many articles there were of this delicate glass. There must have been hundreds of them. But Laura could tell you exactly. She loved each one.

She lived in a world of glass and also a world of music. The music came from a 1920 victrola and a bunch of records that dated from about the same period, pieces such as *Whispering* or *The Love Nest* or *Dardanella*. These records were souvenirs of our father, a man whom we barely remembered, whose name was spoken rarely. Before his sudden and unexplained disappearance from our lives, he had made this gift to the household, the phonograph and the records, whose music remained as a sort of apology for him. Once in a while, on pay-day at the warehouse, I would bring home a new record. But

Laura seldom cared for these new records, maybe because they reminded her too much of the noisy tragedies in Death Valley or the speed-drills at the business college. The tunes she loved were the ones she had always heard. Often she sang to herself at night in her bedroom. Her voice was thin, it usually wandered off-key. Yet it had a curious childlike sweetness. At eight o'clock in the evening I sat down to write in my own mouse-trap of a room. Through the closed doors, through the walls, I would hear my sister singing to herself, a piece like *Whispering* or *I Love You* or *Sleepy Time Gal,* losing the tune now and then but always preserving the minor atmosphere of the music. I think that was why I always wrote such strange and sorrowful poems in those days. Because I had in my ears the wispy sound of my sister serenading her pieces of colored glass, washing them while she sang or merely looking down at them with her vague blue eyes until the points of gem-like radiance in them gently drew the aching particles of reality from her mind and finally produced a state of hypnotic calm in which she even stopped singing or washing the glass and merely sat without motion until my mother knocked at the door and warned her against the waste of electric current.

I don't believe that my sister was actually foolish. I think the petals of her mind had simply closed through fear, and it's no telling how much they had closed upon in the way of secret wisdom. She never talked very much, not even to me, but once in a while she did pop out with something that took you by surprise.

After work at the warehouse or after I'd finished my writing in the evening, I'd drop in her room for a little visit because she had a restful and soothing effect on nerves that were worn rather thin from trying to ride two horses simultaneously in two opposite directions.

I usually found her seated in the straight-back ivory chair with a piece of glass cupped tenderly in her palm.

"What are you doing? Talking to it?" I asked.

"No," she answered gravely, "I was just looking at it."

On the bureau were two pieces of fiction which she had received as Christmas or birthday presents. One was a novel called the *Rose-Garden Husband* by someone whose name escapes me. The other was *Freckles* by Gene Stratton Porter. I never saw her reading the *Rose-Garden Husband,* but the other book was one that she actually lived with. It had probably never occurred to Laura that a book was something you read straight through and then laid aside as finished. The character Freckles, a one-armed orphan youth who worked in a lumber-camp, was someone that she invited into her bedroom now and then for a friendly visit just as she did me. When I came in and found this novel open upon her lap, she would gravely remark that Freckles was having some trouble with the foreman of the lumber-camp or that he had just received an injury to his spine when a tree fell on him. She frowned with genuine sorrow when she reported these misadventures of her story-book hero, possibly not recalling how successfully he came through them all, that the injury to the spine fortuitously resulted in the discovery of rich parents and that the bad-tempered foreman had a heart of gold at the end of the book. Freckles became involved in romance with a girl he called The Angel, but my sister usually stopped reading when this girl became too prominent in the story. She closed the book or turned back to the lonelier periods in the orphan's story. I only remember her making one reference to this heroine of the novel. "The Angel is nice," she said, "but seems to be kind of conceited about her looks."

THEN one time at Christmas, while she was trimming the artificial tree, she picked up the Star of Bethlehem that went on the topmost branch and held it gravely toward the chandelier.

"Do stars have five points really?" she enquired.

This was the sort of thing that you didn't believe and that made you stare at Laura with sorrow and confusion.

"No," I told her, seeing she really meant it, "they're round like the earth and most of them much bigger."

She was gently surprised by this new information. She went to the window to look up at the sky which was, as usual during Saint Louis winters, completely shrouded by smoke.

"It's hard to tell," she said, and returned to the tree.

So TIME passed on till my sister was twenty-three. Old enough to be married, but the fact of the matter was she had never even had a date with a boy. I don't believe this seemed as awful to her as it did to Mother.

At breakfast one morning Mother said to me, "Why

don't you cultivate some nice young friends? How about down at the warehouse? Aren't there some young men down there you could ask to dinner?"

This suggestion surprised me because there was seldom quite enough food on her table to satisfy three people. My mother was a terribly stringent housekeeper, God knows we were poor enough in actuality, but my mother had an almost obsessive dread of becoming even poorer. A not unreasonable fear since the man of the house was a poet who worked in a warehouse, but one which I thought played too important a part in all her calculations.

Almost immediately Mother explained herself.

"I think it might be nice," she said, "for your sister."

I BROUGHT Jim home to dinner a few nights later. Jim was a big red-haired Irishman who had the scrubbed and polished look of well-kept chinaware. His big square hands seemed to have a direct and very innocent hunger for touching his friends. He was always clapping them on your arms or shoulders and they burned through the cloth of your shirt like plates taken out of an oven. He was the best-liked man in the warehouse and oddly enough he was the only one that I was on good terms with. He found me agreeably ridiculous I think. He knew of my secret practice of retiring to a cabinet in the lavatory and working on rhyme schemes when work was slack in the warehouse, and of sneaking up on the roof now and then to smoke my cigarette with a view across the river at the undulant open country of Illinois.

No doubt I was classified as screwy in Jim's mind as much as in the others', but while their attitude was suspicious and hostile when they first knew me, Jim's was warmly tolerant from the beginning. He called me Slim, and gradually his cordial acceptance drew the others around, and while he remained the only one who actually had anything to do with me, the others had now begun to smile when they saw me as people smile at an oddly fashioned dog who crosses their path at some distance.

Nevertheless it took some courage for me to invite Jim to dinner. I thought about it all week and delayed the action till Friday noon, the last possible moment, as the dinner was set for that evening.

"What are you doing tonight?" I finally asked him.

"Not a God damn thing," said Jim. "I had a date but her Aunt took sick and she's hauled her freight to Centralia!"

"Well," I said, "why don't you come over for dinner?"

"Sure!" said Jim. He grinned with astonishing brightness.

I went outside to phone the news to Mother.

Her voice that was never tired responded with an energy that made the wires crackle.

"I suppose he's Catholic?" she said.

"Yes," I told her, remembering the tiny silver cross on his freckled chest.

"Good!" she said. "I'll bake a salmon loaf!"

And so we rode home together in his jalopy.

I had a curious feeling of guilt and apprehension as I

led the lamb-like Irishman up three flights of cracked marble steps to the door of Apartment F, which was not thick enough to hold inside it the odor of baking salmon.

Never having a key, I pressed the bell.

"Laura!" came Mother's voice. "That's Tom and Mr. Delaney! Let them in!"

There was a long, long pause.

"Laura?" she called again. "I'm busy in the kitchen, you answer the door!"

Then at last I heard my sister's footsteps. They went right past the door at which we were standing and into the parlor. I heard the creaking noise of the phonograph crank. Music commenced. One of the oldest records, a march of Sousa's, put on to give her the courage to let in a stranger.

The door came timidly open and there she stood in a dress from Mother's wardrobe, a black chiffon ankle-length and high-heeled slippers on which she balanced uncertainly like a tipsy crane of melancholy plumage. Her eyes stared back at us with a glass brightness and her delicate wing-like shoulders were hunched with nervousness.

"Hello!" said Jim, before I could introduce him.

He stretched out his hand. My sister touched it only for a second.

"Excuse me!" she whispered, and turned with a breathless rustle back to her bedroom door, the sanctuary beyond it briefly revealing itself with the tinkling, muted radiance of glass before the door closed rapidly but gently on her wraithlike figure.

Jim seemed to be incapable of surprise.

"Your sister?" he asked.

"Yes, that was her," I admitted. "She's terribly shy with strangers."

"She looks like you," said Jim, "except she's pretty."

Laura did not reappear till called to dinner. Her place was next to Jim at the drop-leaf table and all through the meal her figure was slightly tilted away from his. Her face was feverishly bright and one eyelid, the one on the side toward Jim, had developed a nervous wink. Three times in the course of the dinner she dropped her fork on her plate with a terrible clatter and she was continually raising the water-glass to her lips for hasty little gulps. She went on doing this even after the water was gone from the glass. And her handling of the silver became more awkward and hurried all the time.

I thought of nothing to say.

To Mother belonged the conversational honors, such as they were. She asked the caller about his home and family. She was delighted to learn that his father had a business of his own, a retail shoe store somewhere in Wyoming. The news that he went to night-school to study accounting was still more edifying. What was his heart set on beside the warehouse? Radio-engineering? My, my, my! It was easy to see that here was a very up-and-coming young man who was certainly going to make his place in the world!

Then she started to talk about her children. Laura, she said, was not cut out for business. She was domestic, however, and making a home was really a girl's best bet.

Jim agreed with all this and seemed not to sense the ghost of an implication. I suffered through it dumbly, trying not to see Laura trembling more and more beneath the incredible unawareness of Mother.

And bad as it was, excruciating in fact, I thought with dread of the moment when dinner was going to be over, for then the diversion of food would be taken away, we would have to go into the little steam-heated parlor. I fancied the four of us having run out of talk, even Mother's seemingly endless store of questions about Jim's home and his job all used up finally — the four of us, then, just sitting there in the parlor, listening to the hiss of the radiator and nervously clearing our throats in the kind of self-consciousness that gets to be suffocating.

But when the blanc-mange was finished, a miracle happened.

Mother got up to clear the dishes away. Jim gave me a clap on the shoulders and said, "Hey, Slim, let's go have a look at those old records in there!"

He sauntered carelessly into the front room and flopped down on the floor beside the victrola. He began sorting through the collection of worn-out records and reading their titles aloud in a voice so hearty that it shot like beams of sunlight through the vapors of self-consciousness engulfing my sister and me.

He was sitting directly under the floor-lamp and all at once my sister jumped up and said to him, "Oh — you have freckles!"

Jim grinned. "Sure that's what my folks call me — Freckles!"

"Freckles?" Laura repeated. She looked toward me as if for the confirmation of some too wonderful hope. I looked away quickly, not knowing whether to feel relieved or alarmed at the turn that things were taking.

Jim had wound the victrola and put on *Dardanella*.

He grinned at Laura.

"How about you an' me cutting the rug a little?"

"What?" said Laura breathlessly, smiling and smiling.

"Dance!" he said, drawing her into his arms.

As far as I knew she had never danced in her life. But to my everlasting wonder she slipped quite naturally into those huge arms of Jim's, and they danced round and around the small steam-heated parlor, bumping against the sofa and chairs and laughing loudly and happily together. Something opened up in my sister's face. To say it was love is not too hasty a judgment, for after all he had freckles and that was what his folks called him. Yes, he had undoubtedly assumed the identity — for all practical purposes — of the one-armed orphan youth who lived in the Limberlost, that tall and misty region to which she retreated whenever the walls of Apartment F became too close to endure.

Mother came back in with some lemonade. She stopped short as she entered the portieres.

"Good heavens! Laura? Dancing?"

Her look was absurdly grateful as well as startled.

"But isn't she stepping all over you, Mr. Delaney?"

"What if she does?" said Jim, with bearish gallantry. "I'm not made of eggs!"

"Well, well, well!" said Mother, senselessly beaming.

"She's light as a feather!" said Jim. "With a little more practice she'd dance as good as Betty!"

There was a little pause of silence.

"Betty?" said Mother.

"The girl I go out with!" said Jim.

"Oh!" said Mother.

She set the pitcher of lemonade carefully down and with her back to the caller and her eyes on me, she asked him just how often he and the lucky young lady went out together.

"Steady!" said Jim.

Mother's look, remaining on my face, turned into a glare of fury.

"Tom didn't mention that you went out with a girl!"

"Nope," said Jim. "I didn't mean to let the cat out of the bag. The boys at the warehouse'll kid me to death when Slim gives the news away."

He laughed heartily but his laughter dropped heavily and awkwardly away as even his dull senses were gradually penetrated by the unpleasant sensation the news of Betty had made.

"Are you thinking of getting married?" said Mother.

"First of next month!" he told her.

It took her several moments to pull herself together. Then she said in a dismal tone, "How nice! If Tom had only told us we could have asked you *both!*"

Jim had picked up his coat.

"Must you be going?" said Mother.

"I hope it don't seem like I'm rushing off," said Jim, "but Betty's gonna get back on the eight o'clock train an' by the time I get my jalopy down to the Wabash depot —"

"Oh, then, we mustn't keep you."

Soon as he'd left, we all sat down, looking dazed.

Laura was the first to speak.

"Wasn't he nice?" she said. "And all those freckles!"

"Yes," said Mother. Then she turned on me.

"You didn't mention that he was engaged to be married!"

"Well, how did I know that he was engaged to be married?"

"I thought you called him your best friend down at the warehouse?"

"Yes, but I didn't know he was going to be married!"

"How peculiar!" said Mother. "How very peculiar!"

"No," said Laura gently, getting up from the sofa. "There's nothing peculiar about it."

She picked up one of the records and blew on its surface a little as if it were dusty, then set it softly back down.

"People in love," she said, "take everything for granted."

What did she mean by that? I never knew.

She slipped quietly back to her room and closed the door.

Not very long after that I lost my job at the warehouse. I was fired for writing a poem on the lid of a shoe-box. I left Saint Louis and took to moving around. The cities swept about me like dead leaves, leaves that were brightly colored but torn away from the branches. My nature changed. I grew to be firm and sufficient.

In five years' time I had nearly forgotten home. I had to forget it, I couldn't carry it with me. But once in a while, usually in a strange town before I have found companions, the shell of deliberate hardness is broken through. A door comes softly and irresistibly open. I hear the tired old music my unknown father left in the place he abandoned as faithlessly as I. I see the faint and sorrowful radiance of the glass, hundreds of little transparent pieces of it in very delicate colors. I hold my breath, for if my sister's face appears among them — the night is hers!

# THE IMPORTANT THING

# THE IMPORTANT

# THING

**T**HEY met at the spring dance by the Baptist Female
College which Flora was attending that year. The college was in the same town as the State University at
which John was completing his sophomore year. He
knew only one girl at the college and wasn't able to find
her in the ballroom. It was hot and crowded in there and
had that feverish, glaring effect which usually prevails at
a spring dance given by a sectarian girls' school. The
room was lighted by four or five blazing chandeliers and
the walls were covered with long mirrors. Between
dances the couples stood about stiffly in their unaccus-
tomed formal dress and glanced uneasily at their reflec-
tions in the highly polished glass, shifted their weight

from foot to foot, nervously twisted or flipped their program cards. None of them seemed to know each other very well. They talked in loud, unnatural voices, shrieked with laughter or stood sullenly quiet. The teachers flitted among them with bird-like alacrity, intently frowning or beaming, introducing, prompting, encouraging. It was not like a social affair. It was more like an important military maneuver.

John walked around the edge of the floor several times and was rather relieved at not finding the one girl he knew. When he arrived at the palm-flanked entrance he turned to go out, but just then his arm was violently plucked by one of the teachers, a middle-aged woman with frowzy grey hair, sharp nose and large yellow teeth. She looked so wild and Harpy-like that John involuntarily squirmed aside from her grasp.

"Are you alone?" she shrieked in his ear.

The band was thumping out a terrifically loud foxtrot. John rubbed his ear and pointed vaguely toward the door. She tightened her grasp on his arm and propelled him across the floor by a series of jerks that careened him from one dancing couple to another till they reached a corner where stood an apparently stranded group of young Baptist Females beneath the protective fronds of an enormous boxed palm.

The Harpy gave his arm a final twist and John found himself facing a tall, thin girl in a pink taffeta dress who stood slightly apart from her fellow refugees. He caught the name Flora shrieked through the increasing din. He didn't notice the girl's face. He was too furious at being roped in like this to even look at her. They advanced awkwardly toward each other. John slid his arm around her unbelievably slender waist. Through the silk he could feel the hard ridge of her spine. There was no weight in her body. She floated before him so lightly that it was almost like dancing by himself, except that the cord of bone kept moving beneath his warm, sweating fingers and her fine, loose hair plastered itself against his damp cheek.

The foxtrot had reached a crescendo. Cymbals were clashing and drums beating out double time. The girl's lips moved against his throat. Her breath tickled his skin but he couldn't hear a word she was saying. He looked helplessly down at her. Suddenly she broke away from him. She stood slightly off from him, her eyes crinkling with laughter and one hand clutched to her mouth. The music stopped.

"What're you laughing at?" John asked.

"The whole situation," said Flora. "You no more wanted to dance than I did!"

"Didn't you want to?"

"Of course not. When I think of dancing I think of Isadora Duncan who said she wanted to teach the whole world how to dance, but this wasn't what she meant — do you think it was?"

She had a way of looking up that made her face very brilliant and for a few moments obscured the fact that she was by no means pretty. But there was something about her, something which already excited him a little, and so he said:

117

"Let's go outside."

They spent practically all the rest of the evening in the oak grove between the gymnasium and the chapel, strolling around and smoking his cigarettes. While smoking the girl would flatten herself against a tree trunk for smoking was forbidden on the campus.

"This is the advantage of being a fence-pole," she told him. "You can hide behind anything with the slightest diameter."

Everything that she said had a wry, humorous twist and even when it wasn't humorous she would laugh slightly and John had the impression that she was unusually clever. They went into the empty chapel for a while and sat in a back pew and talked about religion.

"It is all so archaic," Flora said. "It is all a museum piece!"

John had recently become an agnostic himself. They agreed that Christian religion and Hebrew, in fact nearly all religions were based on a concept of guilt.

"*Mea culpa!*" said John, thinking that she would say, "What's that?" But she didn't. She nodded her head. And he was excited to discover that she, too, was interested in writing. She had won a literary prize in high-school and she was now editor of the college literary magazine. The teacher who had brought them together was Flora's English instructor.

"She thinks I'm very talented," said Flora. "She wants me to send one of my stories to Harper's."

"Why don't you?" asked John.

"Oh, I don't know," said Flora. "I think the main

thing is just expressing yourself as honestly as you can. I am not interested in style," she went on, "it's such a waste of time to do things over and get the right cadence and always just the right word. I'd rather just scramble through one thing and then rush into another, until I have said everything that I have to say!"

How extraordinary it was that she and John should feel exactly the same way about this! He confessed that he was himself a writer and that two or three of his stories were coming out in the University's literary magazine — and when Flora heard this she was almost absurdly moved.

"I'd love to see them, I've got to see them!" she cried.

"I'll bring them over," he promised.

"When?"

"As soon as they come out!"

"I don't care how the style is as long as they're honest. They've got to be honest!" she pleaded. "Are they?"

"I hope so," he answered uneasily.

She had taken his arm and was squeezing it in a grip that was almost as tight as a wrestler's and with every excited inflection in her speech she squeezed it tighter. There was no relaxation in Flora, none of the softness and languor which he found physically interesting in girls. He could not imagine her lying passively still and quietly submitting the way he thought a girl should to a man's embraces.

"What do you think about human relations?" she asked him just at the moment when this disturbing image was in his mind.

"That's a large subject," said John.

"Oh, what a large, large subject! And it is the one I will never be able to cope with!"

"Why?" asked John.

"I'm equal to anything else, but not human relations! I'll always be moving when other people are still, and still when they're moving," said Flora, "and it will be a terrible mess and a mix-up from start to finish!"

"You shouldn't feel that way about it," he told her lamely, astonished at the way her words fitted exactly what he had been thinking.

She looked up at John. "You'll have the same trouble!" she told him. "We'll never be happy but we'll have lots of excitement and if we hold on to our personal integrity everything won't be lost!"

He wasn't quite sure what Flora was talking about, and personal integrity seemed the vaguest of terms. Was it something like what she meant by "honest" writing?

"Yes, something," said Flora, "but ever so much more difficult, because writing is ideal reality and living is not ideal. . . ."

At the window of the gymnasium they stood for a while and watched the dancers who had reached what appeared to be nearly the point of exhaustion. Faces that had been flushed and perspiring when they had left the room were now quite desperate-looking and the men in the jazz-band seemed to be playing now out of sheer inability to break an old habit. Some of the paper streamers had come unfastened and fallen upon the floor, others hung limply from the ceiling and in one corner a small crowd, mostly teachers, were clustered about a girl who had fainted.

"Don't they look silly!" said Flora.

"Who?"

"Dancers — everybody!"

"What isn't silly, in your opinion?" asked John.

"Give me a little while to answer that question!"

"How long shall I give you?"

"I'll tell you right now — The Important Thing isn't silly!"

"What Important Thing?" John asked.

"I don't know yet," said Flora. "Why do you think I'm living, except to discover what The Important Thing is?"

John didn't see her again that spring. Final examinations came soon after the dance, and besides he was not altogether sure that she was the sort he would get along with. She was not good-looking and her intensity which was so charming while he was with her seemed afterwards a little — fantastic!

Very soon after he returned to school that fall he ran into her on the campus. She was now enrolled as a sophomore in the State University. He barely recognized her. It had been so dark in the oak grove, where they spent most of their time at the spring dance, that he hadn't gotten a very clear impression of her face. She was at once homelier and more attractive than he remembered. Her face was very wide at the top and narrow at the bottom: almost an inverted pyramid. Her eyes were large and rather oblique, hazel brown with startling flecks of blue or green in them. Her nose was long and pointed and the tip covered with freckles. She had a way of smiling and blinking her eyes very rapidly as she talked. She talked so fast and shrilly that he felt a little embarrassed. He noticed a group of girls staring at her and giggling. Fools! he thought, and was angry at himself for having felt embarrassed.

It was noon when they met and she was on her way to the boarding-house where she was staying. She hadn't pledged a sorority. She announced the fact with an air of proud defiance that John liked.

"I could see that I wouldn't fit into any of them," she said. "I'd rather be independent, wouldn't you? The trouble with this world is that everybody has to compromise and conform. Oh, I'm sick of it! I won't do it! I shall live my own life just the way that I please!"

John had felt the same way about joining a fraternity and he told her so.

"Ah, we're a couple of Barbs!" she shrieked. "Isn't that marvelous? The other girls at the boarding-house simply detest being called Barbs—but I adore it! I think it's really thrilling to be called a barbarian! It makes you feel like you could strip off your clothes and dance naked in the streets if you felt like doing it!"

John felt a warm glow as though he'd been drinking. It was the way he'd felt in the oak grove, talking to her last spring. It seemed suddenly that he had a great deal to say. He became excited and started talking rapidly about a one-act play that he was writing. It was full of involved symbolism and hard to explain. But Flora nodded her head with quick, eager jerks and supplied words wherever he stumbled. She seemed to know intuitively what he was trying to say.

"Oh, I think that's marvelous, marvelous!" she kept repeating.

He was thinking of submitting it to the one-act play contest. His room-mate had urged him to do so.

"My goodness, why don't you!" exclaimed Flora.

"Oh, I don't know," John said. "I think the main thing is just expressing one's self, don't you?"

Immediately afterwards they both laughed, remembering that Flora had said the same thing about the story her English teacher had wanted her to send to Harper's. "Was it accepted?" John asked.

"No, it came back with a printed card," she admitted ruefully. "But I don't care. I'm writing poetry now. They say that you should write poetry while you're young and feel things keenly."

She laughed and caught John's arm.

"I feel things very keenly, don't you?"

They sat down on the front steps of the boarding-house and talked until the bell tolled for one o'clock classes. Both of them had missed their lunch.

They saw a great deal of each other after that. They had many interests in common. They were both on the staff of the University's literary magazine and belonged to the Poetry and French Clubs. It was the year of the national election and John became twenty-one just in time to vote. Flora spent hours arguing with him about politics and finally convinced him that he must vote for

Norman Thomas. Later they both joined the Young Communists' League. John became a very enthusiastic radical. He helped operate a secret printing press and distribute pamphlets about the campus attacking fraternities, political control of the University, academic conservatism, and so forth. He was once called before the Dean of Men and threatened with expulsion. Flora thought this was terribly thrilling.

"If you get expelled," she promised, "I'll quit school too!"

But it all blew over and they both remained in the University.

All of these things served to draw them closer together. But for some reason they were not altogether at ease with each other. John always had the feeling that something very important was going to happen between them. He could not have explained why he felt that way. Perhaps it was the contagion of Flora's intensity. When he was with her he felt the kind of suppressed excitement a scientist might feel upon the verge of an important discovery. A constant expectation or suspense. Was Flora conscious of the same thing? Sometimes he felt sure that she was. But her enthusiasm was so diffuse that he could never be sure. One thing after another caught her interest. She was like a precocious child just discovering the world, taking nothing in it for granted, receiving each impression with the fresh wonder of a child but an adult's mature understanding. About most things she talked very frankly. But once in a while she would become oddly reticent.

Once he asked her where she came from.

"Kansas," she told him.

"I know, but what place in Kansas?"

He was surprised to see her face coloring. They were in the reference room of the library that evening, studying together at one of the yellow oak tables. She opened her notebook and ignored his question.

"What place?" he insisted, wondering why she flushed.

Abruptly she slammed the notebook shut and faced him with a laugh.

"What does it matter what place?"

"I just wanted to know."

"Well, I won't tell you!"

"Why not?"

"Because it doesn't matter where you come from. It only matters where you're going!"

"Where are you going, then?"

"I don't know!"

She leaned back in the straight yellow oak chair and shook with laughter.

"How on earth should I know where I'm going?"

The librarian approached them with a warning frown.

"Please not so loud. This room's for study."

"Where are you going?" John repeated under his breath.

Flora hid her face in the notebook and continued laughing.

"Where are you going, where are you going, where

are you going!" John whispered. He did it to tease her. She looked so funny with the black leather notebook covering her face, only her braided hair showing and her throat flushed Turkey red.

All at once she jumped up from the table and he saw that her face was contorted with crying. She rushed out of the room and he couldn't get her to speak a word to him all the way back to her boarding-house.

Some time later he found the name of her home town on the envelope of a letter which she'd forgotten to remove from a book of poems she'd loaned him. The envelope was postmarked from Hardwood, Kansas. John grinned. It was a hick town in the northwestern part of the state and probably the deadest spot on earth. . . .

Despising himself for doing so, he opened the letter and read it. It was from Flora's mother and was a classic of its kind. It complained of the money Flora was having to spend on board and books, urged her to spend less time writing nonsense and buckle down to hard work so that she could get a teaching job when she got through with her schooling because times were getting to be very bad. . . .

"The ground and the people and the business and everything else is dried up around here," wrote the mother. "I don't know what things are coming to. It must be God's judgment, I guess. Three solid years of drought. Looks like this time God is planning to dry the wickedness out of the world instead of drowning it out!"

THAT Spring John bought a used car for thirty-five dollars and every free afternoon he and Flora drove around the lovely country roads and had picnic lunches which Flora prepared. He was getting used to Flora's odd appearance and her absurd animation, but other people weren't. She had become something of a "character" on the campus. John was at this time being rushed by a professional fraternity and he was told that some of the fellows thought that Flora was a very queer person for him to be seen around with. Now and again his mind would go back to their first conversation in the oak grove of the Baptist Female College, the talk about human relations and her inability to cope with them, and it appeared to him that she was not even going half way in attempting to. There was no reason for her to talk so loudly on such eclectic subjects whenever they passed along a crowded corridor of a university building, there was surely no reason for her to be so rude to people she wasn't interested in, walking abruptly away without an excuse when talk turned to things she classified as inane—which was almost everything John's other friends talked about.

Other girls on the campus, he could look at and imagine in the future, settled down into average middle-class life, becoming teachers or entering other professions. But when he looked at Flora he could not see her future, he could not imagine her becoming or doing any known thing, or going back to Hardwood, Kansas, or going anywhere else. She did not fit happily or comfortably into the university cosmos but in what other place or circumstances — he asked himself — could she have found any refuge whatsoever? Perhaps he was no more like other people than she was, but his case was different. He was more adaptable, he demanded a good deal less of people and things. Come up against a barrier, he was of a nature to look for a way around it. But Flora —

Flora had decided that the English department of the University was hopelessly reactionary and the only course she took an interest in, now, was geology. Their favorite spot, that spring, was an abandoned rock quarry where Flora searched for fossils. She danced around the quarry like a bright, attractive little monkey on a wire, her green smock fluttering in the wind and her voice constantly flowing up to him, sometimes shrill with excitement and sometimes muted with intense absorption.

"Don't you ever want to be still?" John asked her.

"Never till I have to!"

John would get tired of waiting and would open the lunch-box. She would finally join him on the hill-top, too tired to eat, and would spread her fossils around her and pore delightedly over them while John munched sandwiches of peanut butter and jelly or swiss cheese on rye. The rest of the afternoon they would spend talking about literature and life, art and civilization. They both had tremendous admiration for the ancient Greeks and the modern Russians. Greece is the world's past, said Flora, and Russia is the future — which John thought a brilliant statement, though it sounded a little familiar as if he had come across it somewhere before in a book.

Their discussions would continue unflaggingly till sundown, but as dusk began to settle they would become a little nervous and constrained, for some reason, and there would be long pauses in their talk, during which it was curiously difficult for them to look at each other. After a while, when it was getting really dark, Flora would abruptly jump up from the grass and brush off her smock.

"I guess we'd better be going," she would say. Her voice would sound with the dull, defeated tone of someone who has argued a long time about something very important without making any impression upon the other's mind. John would feel strangely miserable as he followed her down the hill to where they had parked the old roadster. He would also feel that something had been left unsaid or undone, a feeling of incompletion....

It was the last Saturday before the end of the spring term. They were going to spend the whole day out in the country, studying for a final examination in a French course which they were taking together. Flora had prepared sandwiches and deviled eggs. And John, with some trepidation, had purchased a quart of red wine. He put the bottle in the side pocket of the roadster and didn't mention it until after they'd finished eating because he knew Flora didn't like drinking. She had no moral objections, she said, but thought it was a senseless, wasteful practice. She refused to drink any of the wine. "But you may, if you wish," she added with a primness that made John laugh.

They were seated as usual on the grassy hill above the rock quarry. It was called Lover's Leap. Flora held the notebook which they had prepared together and was quizzing John. She was leaning against one of the large white boulders scattered about the hill-top and John was stretched at her feet. He held the wine bottle between his knees and drank out of the thermos cup. Flora's constraint at first sight of the bottle wore off. She called him Bacchus.

"I wish I had time to make you a wreath," she said. "You'd look too adorable with a wreath of green leaves!"

"Why don't you be a nymph?" John asked. "Take off your clothes and be a wood nymph! I'll chase you through the birch trees!"

The idea pleased John very much. He laughed loudly. But Flora was embarrassed. She cleared her throat and held the notebook in front of her face, but he could see by the base of her throat that she was blushing. He stopped laughing, feeling somewhat embarrassed himself. He knew what she was thinking. She was thinking what might happen if he should catch her among the birch trees with all her clothes off. . . .

John drank another cupful of wine. He felt very good. He had removed his jacket and unbuttoned the collar of his shirt and rolled up the sleeves. The sun shone dazzlingly in his eyes, made rainbows in his eyelashes, warmed the bare flesh of his throat and arms. A comfortable glow passed through him. He was newly conscious of the life in his body; flexed his legs, rubbed his stomach and arched his thighs. He no longer listened to the questions that Flora was asking him out of the notebook. She had to repeat them two or three times before they were clear.

At last she became disgusted and tossed the notebook aside.

"I believe you're getting intoxicated!" she told him sharply.

He looked indolently up at her.

"Maybe I am! What of it?"

He noticed that she was not very pretty. Especially not when she drew her brows together and squinted her eyes like that. Her face was irregular and bony-looking. Rather outlandish. So broad at the top and narrow at the bottom. Long pointed nose, and eyes, flecked with different colors, which were too large for the rest of her and always so filled with superfluous brightness. Reminded him of an undersized child he once knew in grammar school. For some reason they called him Peekie and threw rocks at him after school. A timid, ridiculous creature with a high, squeaky voice that everyone mocked. The large boys caught him after school and asked him the meaning of obscene words or pulled the buttons off his knickers. She was like that. A queer person. But there was something exciting about her just as there'd been something exciting about Peekie that made the larger boys want to amuse themselves with him. There was something about her that he wanted to set his hands on in a rough way — twist and pull and tease! Her skin was the most attractive thing about her. It was very fine and smooth and white. . . .

John's eyes traveled down her body. She wore a black sweater and a black and white checked skirt. As he looked at her legs a brisk wind tossed the skirt up and he could see the bare flesh above where the stockings ended. He rolled over on his stomach and placed both hands on her thighs. He'd never touched her so intimately before but somehow it seemed a perfectly natural thing to do. She made a startled movement away from him. Suddenly he thought he knew what the important thing was that was going to happen between them. He caught her by the shoulders and tried to pull her down in the grass, but she fought against him wildly. Neither of them said anything. They just fought together like two wild animals, rolling in the grass and clawing at each other. Flora clawed at John's face and John clawed at Flora's body. They accepted this thing, this desperate battle between them, as though they'd known all along it was coming, as though it had been inevitable from the start. Neither of them spoke a word until they were at last exhausted and lay still on the grass, breathing heavily and looking up at the slowly darkening sky.

John's face was scratched and bleeding in several places. Flora pressed her hands against her stomach and groaned. He had kicked her with his knee trying to make her lie still.

"It's all over now," he said. "I'm not going to hurt you." But she continued moaning.

The sun had gone down and dusk gathered. There was a big purplish red blotch in the western sky that looked like a bruised place.

John got up to his feet and stood silently staring at the angry afterglow. A way off to the left was the university town, beginning to emerge through its leafy clouds with the sparkling animation of a Saturday night in late spring. There would be many gay parties and dances that night. Girls in dresses that seemed to be woven of flowers would whirl about polished dance-floors and couples would whisper and laugh behind clumps of ghostly spirea. These were the natural celebrations of youth. He and this girl had been searching for something else. What was it? Again and again later on the search would be made, the effort to find something outside of common experience, digging and rooting among the formless rubble of things for the one lost thing that was altogether lovely — and perhaps every time a repetition of this, violence and ugliness of desire turned to rage....

He spoke aloud to himself. "We didn't have anything — we were fooling ourselves."

He turned from the dark, haunting beauty of the town and looked down at Flora. She blinked her eyes and drew her breath sharply. She looked almost ugly, her face covered with sweat and grass stain. She was not like a girl. He wondered that he had never noticed before how anonymous was her gender, for this was the very central fact of her nature. She belonged nowhere, she fitted in no place at all, she had no home, no shell, no place of comfort or refuge, she was a fugitive with no place to run to. Others in her position might make some adjustment. The best of whatever is offered, however not right. But Flora would not accept it, none of the ways and means. The most imperfect part of her was the most pure. And that meant —

"Flora. . . ."

He held out his hand and put his heart in his eyes. She felt the sudden turning of understanding and took his hand and he pulled her gently to her feet.

For the first time they stood together in the dark without any fear of each other, their hands loosely clasped and returning each other's look with sorrowful understanding, unable to help each other except through knowing, each completely separate and alone — but no longer strangers. . . .

# THE ANGEL IN
# THE ALCOVE

# THE ANGEL IN
# THE ALCOVE

SUSPICION is the occupational disease of landladies and long association with them has left me with
an obscure sense of guilt I will probably never be free of.
The initial trauma in this category was inflicted by a
land-lady I had in the old French Quarter of New
Orleans when I was barely twenty. She was the archetype of the suspicious land-lady. She had a room of her
own but preferred to sleep on a rattling cot in the downstairs hall so that none of her tenants could enter or leave
the establishment during the night without her grudg-
ing permission. When finally I left there I fooled the old
woman. I left by way of a balcony and a pair of sheets.

I was miles out of town on the Old Spanish Trail to the West before the old woman found out I had gotten past her.

The downstairs hall of this rooming-house on Bourbon Street was totally lightless. You had to grope your way through it with cautious revulsion, trailing your fingers along the damp, cracked plaster until you arrived at the door or the foot of the stairs. You never reached either without the old woman's challenge. Her ghostly figure would spring bolt upright on the rattling iron cot. She would utter one syllable — *Who?* If she were not satisfied with the identification given, or suspected that you were taking your luggage out in a stealthy departure or bringing somebody in for carnal enjoyment, a match would be struck on the floor and held toward you for several moments. In its weirdly flickering light she would squint her eyes at you until her doubts were dismissed. Then she would flop back down in a huddle of sour blankets and if you waited to listen you would hear mutterings vicious and coarse as any that drunks in Quarter bar-rooms ever gave voice to.

She was a woman of paranoidal suspicion and her suspicion of me was unbounded. Often she came in my room with the morning paper and read aloud some item concerning an act of crime in the Quarter. After the reading she would inspect me closely for any guilty change of countenance, and I would nearly always gratify her suspicion with a deep flush and inability to return her look. I am sure she had chalked up dozens of crimes against me and was only waiting for some more concrete betrayal to call the police, a captain of whom, she had warned me, was her first cousin.

The land-lady was a victim of dead beats, that much should be admitted in her defense. None of her tenants were regular payers. Some of them clung to their rooms for months and months with only promises given of future payment. One of these was a widow named Mrs. Wayne. Mrs. Wayne was the most adroit sponger in the house. She even succeeded in finagling gratuities from the land-lady. Her fortune was in her tongue. She was a wonderful raconteur of horribly morbid or salacious stories. Whenever she smelled food cooking her door would fly open and she would dart forth with a mottled blue and white sauce-pan held to her bosom coquettishly as a lace fan. Undoubtedly she was half starved and the odor of food set her off like a powerful drug, for there was an abnormal brilliance in her chatter. She tapped on the door from which the seductive smell came but entered before there could be any kind of response. Her tongue would be off before she was fairly inside and no amount of rudeness short of forcible ejection from the room would suffice to discourage her. There was something pitifully winning about the old lady. Even her bad-smelling breath became a component of her unwholesome appeal. To me it was the spectacle of so much heroic vitality in so wasted a vessel that warmed my heart toward the widow. I never did any cooking in my attic bedroom. I only met Mrs. Wayne in the land-lady's kitchen on those occasions when I had earned my supper by some small job on the premises. The land-lady herself was not entirely immune to Mrs. Wayne's charm and the stories unmistakably entranced her. As she put things on the stove she would always remark, If the bitch gets a sniff of this cookin' wild horses won't hold 'er!

In eight years' time such characters disappear, the earth swallows them up, the walls absorb them like moisture. Undoubtedly old Mrs. Wayne and her battered utensil have made their protesting departure and I am not at all sure that with them the world has not lost the greatest pathological genius since Baudelaire or Poe. Her favorite subject was the deaths of relatives and friends which she had attended with an eye and ear from which no agonizing detail escaped annotation. Her memory served them up in the land-lady's kitchen so graphically that I would find myself sick with horror and yet so fascinated that the risk of losing my appetite for a hard-earned supper would not prevail upon me to shut my ears. The land-lady was equally spell-bound. Gradually her gruff mumblings of disbelief and impatient gestures would give way to such morbid enjoyment that her jaws would slacken and dribble. A faraway mesmerized look would come into her usually pin-sharp eyes. All the while Mrs. Wayne with the sauce-pan held to her bosom would be executing a slow and oblique approach to the great kitchen stove. So powerful was her enchantment that even when she was actually removing the lid from the stew-pot and ladling out some of its contents into her sauce-pan, although the land-lady's look would follow her movements there would not appear to be any recognition. Not until the hapless protagonist of the story had endured his final conclusion — his eyeballs popped from their sockets and ghastly effluvia drenching his bed-clothes — did the charm loosen enough to permit the narrator's listeners any clear knowledge of what went on outside the scene that was painted. By that time Mrs. Wayne had scraped her sauce-pan clean with wolfish relish and made her way so close to the door that if any unpleasantness attended the land-lady's emergence from trance, the widow could be out of ear-shot before it achieved a momentum.

In this old house it was either deathly quiet or else the high plaster walls were ringing like fire-bells with angry voices, with quarrels over the use of the lavatory or accusations of theft or threats of eviction. I had no door to my room which was in the attic, only a ragged curtain that couldn't exclude the barrage of human wretchedness often exploding. The walls of my room were pink and green stippled plaster and there was an alcove window. This alcove window shone faintly in the night. There was a low bench beneath it. Now and again when the room was otherwise lightless a misty grey figure would appear to be seated on this bench in the alcove. It was the tender and melancholy figure of an angel or some dim, elderly madonna. The apparition occurred in the alcove most often on those winter nights in New Orleans when slow rain is falling from a sky not clouded heavily enough to altogether separate the town from the moon. New Orleans and the moon have always seemed to me to have an understanding between them, an intimacy of sisters grown old together, no longer needing more than a speechless look to communicate their feelings to each other. This lunar atmosphere of the city draws me back whenever the waves of energy which removed me to more vital towns have spent themselves and a time of recession is called for. Each time I have felt some rather profound psychic wound, a loss or a failure, I have returned to this city. At such periods I would seem to belong there and no place else in the country.

During this first period in New Orleans none of the small encouragements in my life as a writer had yet come along and I had already accepted the terms of anonymity and failure. I had already learned to make a religion of endurance and a secret of my desperation. The nights were comforting. When the naked lightbulb had been turned off and everything visible gone except the misty alcove set deeply and narrowly into the wall above Bourbon, I would seem to slip into another state of being which had no trying associations with the world. For a while the alcove would remain empty, just a recess that light came faintly into: but after my thoughts had made some dreamy excursion or other and I turned again to look in that direction, the transparent figure would noiselessly have entered and seated herself on the bench below the window and begun that patient watching which put me to sleep. The hands of the figure were folded among the colorless draperies of her lap and her eyes were fixed up on me with a gentle, unquestioning look which I came to remember as having belonged to my grandmother during her sieges of illness when I used to go to her room and sit by her bed and want to say something or put my hand over hers but could not do either, knowing that if I did I would burst into tears that would trouble her more than her illness.

The appearance of this grey figure in the alcove never preceded the time of falling asleep by more than a few moments. When I saw her there I thought comfortably, Ah, now, I'm about to slip away, it will all be gone in a moment and won't come back until morning. . . .

On one of those nights a more substantial visitor came to my room. I was jolted out of sleep by a warmth that was not my own, and I awoke to find that someone had entered my room and was crouching over the bed. I jumped up and nearly cried out, but the arms of the visitor passionately restrained me. He whispered his name which was that of a tubercular young artist who slept in the room adjoining. I want to, I want to, he whispered. So I lay back and let him do what he wanted until he was finished. Then without any speech he got up and left my room. For a while afterwards I heard him coughing and muttering to himself through the wall between us. Turbulent feelings were on both sides of that wall. But at last I was drowsy again. I cocked an eye toward the alcove. Yes, she was there. I wondered if she had witnessed the strange goings-on and what her attitude was toward perversions of longing. But nothing gave any sign. The two weightless hands so loosely clasping each other among the colorless draperies of the lap, the cool and believing grey eyes in the faint pearly

face, were immobile as statuary. I felt that she had per-
mitted the act to occur and had neither blamed nor
approved, and so I went off to sleep.

NOT long after the episode in my room the artist was
involved in a terrible scene with the land-lady. His
disease was entering the final stage, he coughed all the
time but managed to go on working. He was a quick-
sketch artist at the Court of the Two Parrots which was
around the corner on Toulouse. He did not trust anybody or anything. He lived in a world completely hostile
to him, unrelentingly hostile, and no other being could
enter the walls about him for more than the frantic
moments desire drove him to. He would not give in to
the mortal fever which licked all the time at his nerves.
He invented all sorts of trivial complaints and grudges
to hide from himself the knowledge that he was dying.
One of these subterfuges to which he resorted was a
nightly preoccupation with bed-bugs. He claimed that
his mattress was infested with them, and every morning
he made an angry report to the land-lady on the number
that had bitten him during the night. These numbers
grew and grew to appalling figures. The old woman
wouldn't believe him. Finally one morning he did get
her into the room to take a look at the bed-clothes.

I heard him breathing hoarsely while the old woman
shuffled and rattled about the corner his bed was in.

Well, she finally grunted, I ain't found nothin'.

Christ, said the artist, you're blind!

Okay! You show me! What is there on this bed?

Look at that! said the artist.

What?

That spot of blood on the pillow.

Well?

That's where I smashed a bed-bug as big as my thumb-nail!

Ho, ho, ho, said the land-lady. That's where you spit up blood!

There was a pause in which his breathing grew hoarser. His speech when it burst out again was dreadfully altered.

How dare you, God damn you, say that!

Ho, ho, ho! I guess you claim you never spit up no blood?

No, no, never! he shouted.

Ho, ho, ho! You spit up blood all the time. I've seen your spit on the stairs and in the hall and on the floor of this bedroom. You leave a trail of it everywhere that you go, a bloody track like a chicken that runs with its head off. You hawk and you spit and you spread contamination. And that ain't all that you do by a long shot neither!

*Now,* yelled the artist — What kind of a dirty insinuation is *that*?

Ho, ho, ho! Insinuation of nothin' but what's known facts!

Get out! he shouted.

I'm in my own house and I'll say what I want where I please! I know all about you degenerates in the Quarter. I ain't let rooms ten years in the Quarter for nothin'. A bunch of rotten half breeds and drunks an' degenerates, that's what I've had to cope with. But you're the worst of the bunch, barring none! And it's not just here but at the Two Parrots, too. Your awful condition's become the main topic of talk at the place where you work. You spit all around your easel in the courtyard. It's to be mopped with a strong disinfectant each night. The management is disgusted. They wish you would fold up your easel and get to hell out. They only don't ask you because you're a pitiful case. Why, one of the waitresses told me some customers left without paying their bill because you was hawking and spitting right next to their table. That's how it is, and the management's fed up with it!

You're making up lies!

It's God's own truth! I got it from the cashier!

I ought to hit you!

Go on!

I ought to knock your ugly old lying face in!

Go on, go on, just try it! I got a nephew that's a captain on the police force! Hit me an you'll land smack in the House of Detention! A rubber hose on your back is what you'll git in there!

I ought to twist those dirty lies out of your neck!

Ho, ho, just try it! Even the effort would kill you!

You'll be punished, he gasped. One of these nights you'll get a knife stuck in you!

By you, I suppose? Ho, ho! You'll die on the street, you'll cough up your lungs in the gutter! You'll go to the morgue. Nobody will claim that skinny cadaver of yours. You'll go in a box and be dumped off a barge in the river. The sooner the better is how I look at it, too. A case like you is a public nuisance and danger. You've got no right to expose healthy people to you. You ought to go into the charity ward at Saint Vincent's. That is the place for a person in dying condition who ain't got the sense to know what is really wrong with him but goes about raising a stink about bugs putting blood on his pillow. Huh! Bugs! You're the bugs that puts blood all over this linen! It's you, not bugs, that makes such a filthy mess at the Court of Two Parrots it's got to be scoured with lye when you leave ev'ry night! It's you, not bugs, that drives the customers off without paying their checks. The management's not disgusted with bugs, but with you! And if you don't leave of your own sweet accord pretty quick you'll be given y'ur notice. And I'm not keepin' yuh neither. Not after y'ur threats an' the scene that you've made this mawnin'. I want you to gather all of y'ur old junk up, all of y'ur dirty old hand-kerchiefs an' y'ur bottles, and get 'em all out of here by twelve o'clock noon, or by God, an' by Jesus, anything that's left here is going straight down to the incinerator! I'll gather it up on the end of a ten-foot pole and dump it into the fire, cause nothing you touch is safe for human contact!

He ran from the room, I heard him running down-stairs and out of the building. I went to the alcove win-dow and watched him spinning wildly around in the street. He was crazed with fury. A waiter from the Chinese restaurant came out and caught at his arm, a drunk from a bar reasoned with him. He sobbed and lamented and wandered from door to door of the ancient buildings until the drunk had maneuvered him into a bar.

The land-lady and a fat old Negress who worked on the place removed the young man's mattress from his bed and lugged it into the courtyard. They stuffed it into the iron pit of the incinerator and set it afire and stood at respectful distance watching it burn. The land-lady wasn't content with just the burning, she made a long speech at the top of her voice about it.

It's not bein' burned because of no bugs, she shouted. I'm burnin' this mattress because it's contaminated. A T.B. case has been on it, a filthy degenerate and a liar!

She went on and on until the mattress was fully consumed, and after.

Then the old Negress was sent upstairs to remove the young man's belongings. It had begun to rain and despite the land-lady's objections the Negress put all of the things beneath the banana tree in the courtyard and covered them with a discarded sheet of linoleum weighted down with loose bricks.

At sun-down the young man returned to the place. I heard him coughing and gasping in the rainy courtyard as he collected his things from under the fantastic green and yellow umbrella of the banana tree. He seemed to be talking about all the wrongs he had suffered since he had come into the world, but at last the complaints were centered upon the loss of a handsome comb. Oh, my God, he muttered, She's stolen my comb, I had a beautiful comb that I got from my mother, a tortoiseshell comb with a silver and pearl handle on it. That's gone, it's been stolen, the comb that belonged to my mother!

At last it was found, or the young man gave up the search, for his talk died out. A wet silver hush fell over the house on Bourbon as daylight and rain both ended their business there, and in my room the luminous dial of a clock and the misty grey of the alcove were all that remained for me of the visible world.

The episode put an end to my stay at the house. For several nights after that the transparent grey angel failed to appear in the alcove and sleep had to come without any motherly sanction. So I decided to give up my residence there. I felt that the delicate old lady angel had tacitly warned me to leave, and that if I ever was visited by her again, it would be at another time in another place — which still haven't come.

# THE FIELD OF
# BLUE CHILDREN

# THE FIELD OF BLUE CHILDREN

**T**HAT final spring at the State University a restlessness came over Myra which she could not understand. It was not merely the restlessness of superabundant youth. There was something a little neurotic about it. Nothing that she did seemed quite satisfying or complete. Even when she returned from a late formal dance, where she had swung from partner to partner the whole evening through, she did not feel quite ready to tumble exhausted into bed. She felt as though there must be something still further to give the night its perfect fullness. Sometimes she had the almost panicky sensation of having lost or forgotten something very important. She would stand quite still for a moment with tightened forehead, trying to remember just what it was that had slipped from her fingers — been left behind in the rumble seat of Kirk's roommate's roadster or on the sofa in the dimly-lighted fraternity lounge between dances.

"What's the matter?" Kirk or somebody else would ask and she would laugh rather sharply.

"Nothing. I just felt like I'd forgotten something!"

The feeling persisted even when every article was accounted for. She still felt as though something were missing. When she had returned to the sorority house she went from room to room, exchanging anecdotes of the evening, laughing at them far more than their humor warranted. And when finally everyone else had gone to bed, she stayed up alone in her room and sometimes she cried bitterly without knowing why, crushing the pillow against her mouth so that no one could hear — or else she sat in pajamas on the window seat and looked out across the small university town with all its buildings and trees and open fields a beautiful dusky blue in the spring night, the dome of the administration building like a snowy peak in the distance and the stars astonishingly large and close — she felt as though she would strangle with an emotion whose exact nature or meaning she could not understand.

When half-drunken groups of serenaders, also restless after late dances, paused beneath her house, she turned on the bed lamp and leaned above them, patting her hands together in a pantomime of delighted applause. When they left, she remained at the window, looking out with the light extinguished, and it was sad, unbearably sad, to hear their hoarse voices retreating down moon-splashed avenues of trees till they could not be heard any longer or else were drowned in the noise of a starting motor whose raucous gravel-kicking departure ebbed quickly to a soft, musical hum and was succeeded at length by the night's complete blue silence.

Still seated at the window, she waited with tight throat for the sobbing to commence. When it did, she felt better. When it did not, her vigil would sometimes continue till morning began and the restless aching had worn itself out.

That spring she took Kirk Abbott's fraternity pin. But this did not radically change her manner of living. She continued to accept dates with other men. She went out almost wherever she was asked with almost whoever asked her, and when Kirk protested she didn't try to explain the fever that made her behave in this way, she simply kissed him until he stopped talking and was in a mood to forgive her for almost anything that she might conceivably do.

From the beginning of adolescence, perhaps earlier, Myra had written a little verse. But this spring it became a regular practice. Whenever the rising well of unexplainable emotion became so full that its hurt was intolerable, she found that it helped her a little to scribble things down on paper. Single lines or couplets, sometimes whole stanzas, leapt into her mind with the instant completeness of slides flashed on the screen of a magic lantern. Their beauty startled her: sometimes it was like a moment of religious exaltation. She stood in a frozen attitude; her breath was released in a sigh. Each time she felt as though she were about to penetrate some new area of human thought. She had the sensation of standing upon the verge of a shadowy vastness which might momentarily flower into a marvelous crystal of light, like a ballroom that is dark one moment and is the next moment illuminated by the sunlike brilliance of a hundred glass chandeliers and reflecting mirrors and polished floors. At such times she would turn out the light in her bedroom and go quickly to the window. When she looked out across the purple-dark town and the snowy white dome above the quadrangle, or when she sat as in a spell, listening to the voices that floated down the quiet streets, singers of blues-songs or laughing couples in roadsters, the beauty of it no longer tormented her, she felt instead a mysterious quietness as though some disturbing question had been answered and life had accordingly become a much simpler and more pleasurable experience.

*"Words are a net to catch beauty!"*

She wrote this in the back of a notebook toward the close of a lecture on the taxing powers of Congress. It was late in April when she wrote this — and from then on it seemed that she understood what she wanted and the hurt bewilderment in her grew less acute.

In the Poetry Club to which Myra belonged there was a boy named Homer Stallcup who had been in love with her for a year or more. She could tell this by the way that he looked at her during the club sessions, which were the

BLUE CHILDREN

only occasions on which they met. Homer never looked directly at her, his eyes slid quickly across her face, but something about his expression, even about the tense pose of his body as he sat gripping his knees, made her feel his awareness of her. He avoided sitting next to her or even directly across from her — the chairs were usually arranged in a circle — and because of this she had at first thought that he must dislike her, but she had come gradually to understand that his shyness toward her had an exactly opposite meaning.

Homer was not a fraternity member. He waited on tables at a campus restaurant, fired furnaces and did chores for his room and board. Nobody in Myra's social *milieu* knew him or paid him any attention. He was rather short, stocky and dark. Myra thought him good-looking, but certainly not in any usual way. He had intense black eyes, a straight nose with flaring nostrils, full, mobile lips that sometimes jerked nervously at the corners. All of his movements were overcharged. When he rose from a chair he would nearly upset it. When he lighted a cigarette his face would twist into a terrible scowl and he would fling the burnt match away like a lighted firecracker.

He went around a great deal with a girl of his own intellectual type, a girl named Hertha something or other, who was rather widely known on the campus because of her odd behavior. In classes she would be carried away by enthusiasm upon some subject, either literary or political, and she would talk so rapidly that nobody could understand what she was saying and she would

157

splutter and gasp and make awkward gestures — as though she were trying to pluck some invisible object out of the air — till the room was in an uproar of amusement and the instructor had to turn his face to the blackboard to conceal his own laughter.

Hertha and this boy, Homer, made a queer picture together, she nearly a foot taller, often rushing along a foot or more in advance of him, clutching him by the coat sleeve as though afraid that he might escape from her, and every minute or so one or both of them bursting into violent laughter that could be heard for a block.

Homer wrote poetry of a difficult sort. It was uneven. Parts of it were reminiscent of Hart Crane, parts were almost as naïvely lucid as Sara Teasdale's. But there were lines and phrases which stabbed at you with their poignant imagery, their fresh observation. When he had given a reading at a symposium, Hertha would always leap out of her chair as though animated by an electric charge, her blinking, near-sighted eyes tensely sweeping the circle of superciliously smiling faces, first demanding, then begging that they concur in the extravagant praise which her moist lips babbled. Only Myra would say anything when Hertha had finished. The rest were too baffled or too indifferent or even too hostile. And Homer's face, darkly flushed, would be turned to his lap throughout the rest of the meeting. His fingers would fold down corners of the neat pages as though the poetry had been erased from them or had never been written on them, as though these pages were simply blank pieces of paper for his fingers to play with.

Myra always wanted to say something more, but her critical vocabulary was slight.

"I think that was lovely," she would say. Or "I liked that very much." And Homer would not lift his eyes, his face would turn even darker, and she would bite her tongue as though in remorse for an unkind speech. She wanted to put her hands over his fingers, to make them stop crumpling the neat pages, to make them be still.

IT WAS not till the last meeting of the year, in early June, that Myra had the courage to approach him. After that meeting she saw him standing by the water fountain at the end of the corridor. She rushed impulsively up to him and told him, all in one breath, that his was the best unpublished verse she'd ever heard, that he should submit it to some of the good literary magazines, that she thought the other members of the club were absolute fools for not understanding.

Homer stood with his fists clenched in his pockets. He did not look at her face the whole time she was speaking. When she had stopped, his excitement burst through. He tore a sheaf of manuscripts from his brief case and thrust them into her hands.

"Please read them," he begged, "and let me know what you think."

They went downstairs together. On the bottom step he tripped or slid and she had to catch his arm to prevent him from falling. She was both touched and amused by this awkwardness and by his apparent delight in walking beside her. As they went out of the white stone building the late afternoon sun, yellow as lemon, met their faces in a beneficent flood. The air was filled with the ringing of five-thirty bells and the pliant voices of pigeons. A white feather from one of the stirring wings floated down and lighted upon Myra's hair. Homer lifted it off and thrust it in his hatband, and all the way home, after leaving him, Myra could feel that quick, light touch of his fingers. She wondered if he would keep the pigeon's feather; treasure it, possibly, for a long while afterward because it had once touched her person.

THAT night, when the sorority house was submerged in darkness, she took out the sheaf of poems and read them through without stopping. As she read she felt a rising excitement. She did not understand very much of what she was reading, but there was a cumulative effect, a growing intensity in the sequence. When she had finished she found herself trembling: trembling as when you step from warm water into chill air.

She dressed and went downstairs. She didn't know what she was planning to do. Her movements were without any conscious direction. And yet she had never moved with more certainty.

She opened the front door of the sorority house, ran down the brick-paved walk, turned to the left and continued swiftly through the moonlit streets till she had reached Homer's residence. It startled her to find herself there. There were cicadas burring in the large oaks — she had not heard them until this moment. And when she looked upward she saw a close group of stars above the western gable of the large frame house. The Seven Sisters. They were huddled together like virgin wanderers through a dark forest. She listened and there was not a voice anywhere, nothing except the chant of cicadas and the faint, faint rustling of her white skirt when she moved.

She went quickly around the side of the house to the door that she had seen Homer come out of in the mornings. She gave two short, distinct raps, then flattened herself against the brick wall. She was breathing rapidly. After waiting a while, she knocked again. Through the glass pane she could see down a flight of stairs into the basement. The door of a lamplit room was open. She saw first a moving shadow, then the boy himself, catching a heavy brown robe about his body and frowning up at the door as he mounted toward it.

As the door came open she gasped his name.

For a whole minute, it seemed, he said nothing. Then he caught her arm and pulled her inside the door.

"Myra, it's you."

"Yes, it's me," she laughed. "I don't know what came over me. I've been reading your poetry and I just felt like I had to see you at once and tell you...."

Her breath gave out. She leaned against the closed door. It was her eyes this time, and not his, that looked for concealment. She looked down at the bottom of his ugly brown bathrobe and she saw his bare feet beneath it, large and bony and white, and the sight of them frightened her. She remembered the intense, fleeting way of his eyes sliding over her face and body and the way he trembled that afternoon when she came up to him in the corridor, how those large feet had tripped on the bottom stair and she had been forced to catch him to keep him from falling.

"There was one thing in particular," she went on with a struggle. "There was something about a field of blue flowers. . . . "

"Oh, yes," he whispered. "The blue children, you mean!"

"Yes, that was it!" Now she lifted her eyes, eagerly.

"Come down to my room, Myra."

"I couldn't!"

"You couldn't?"

"No, of course not! If anyone caught me. . . . "

"They wouldn't!"

"I'd be expelled!"

There was a slight pause.

"Wait a minute!"

He ran down three steps and turned.

"Wait for me just one minute, Myra!"

She felt her head nodding. She heard his running down the rest of the steps and into the basement room where he lived. Through the door she saw his shadow moving about the floor and the walls. He was dressing. Once he stepped into the portion of the bedroom that she could see through the half-open door and he stood in her sight naked from the waist up, and she was startled and strangely moved by that brief glimpse of his full, powerful chest and arms, strikingly etched with shadows thrown by the lamp. In that moment he acquired in her mind a physical reality which he had never had before. A very great physical reality, greater than she had felt in Kirk Abbott or in any of the other young men that she had gone with on the campus.

A minute later he stepped out of the door and closed it and came quietly up the short flight of steps to where she was standing.

"I'm sorry I took so long."

"It wasn't long."

He took her arm and they went out of the door and around to the front of the house. The oak tree in the front lawn appeared gigantic. Everything was peculiarly sharpened or magnified; even the crunch of gravel under their two pairs of white shoes. She expected to see startled, balloon-like heads thrust out of all the upstairs windows, to hear voices calling a shrill alarm, her name shouted from rooftops, the rushing of crowds in pursuit. . . .

"Where are we going?" she asked as he led her south along the brick walk.

"I want to show you the field I describe in the poem."

It wasn't far. The walk soon ended and under their feet was the plushy coolness of earth. The moon flowed aqueously through the multitude of pointed oak leaves: the dirt road was also like moving water with its variations of light and shade. They came to a low wooden fence. The boy jumped over it. Then held out his arms. She stepped to the top rail and he lifted her down from it. On the other side his arms did not release her but held her closer.

"This is it," he told her, "the field of blue children."

She looked beyond his dark shoulder. And it was true. The whole field was covered with dancing blue flowers. There was a wind scudding through them and they broke before it in pale blue waves, sending up a soft whispering sound like the infinitely diminished crying of small children at play.

She thought of the view from her window at night, those nights when she cried bitterly without knowing why, the dome of the administration building like a white peak and the restless waves of moonlit branches and the stillness and the singing voices, mournfully remote, blocks away, coming closer, the tender, foolish ballads, and the smell of the white spirea at night, and the stars clear as lamps in the cloud-fretted sky, and she remembered the choking emotion that she didn't understand and the dread of all this coming to its sudden, final conclusion in a few months or weeks more. And she tightened her arms about the boy's shoulders. He was almost a stranger. She knew that she had not even caught a first glimpse of him until this night, and yet he was inexpressibly close to her now, closer than she had ever felt any person before.

He led her out over the field where the flowers rose in pale blue waves to her knees and she felt their soft petals against her bare flesh and she lay down among them and stretched her arms through them and pressed her lips against them and felt them all about her, accepting her and embracing her, and a kind of drunkenness possessed her. The boy knelt beside her and touched her cheek with his fingers and then her lips and her hair. They were both kneeling in the blue flowers, facing each other. He was smiling. The wind blew her loose hair into his face. He raised both hands and brushed it back over her forehead and as he did so his hands slipped down behind the back of her head and fastened there and drew her head toward him until her mouth was pressed against his, tighter and tighter, until her teeth pressed painfully against her upper lip and she tasted the salt taste of blood. She gasped and let her mouth fall open and then she lay back among the whispering blue flowers.

AFTERWARD she had sense enough to see that it was impossible. She sent the poems back to the boy with a short note. It was a curiously stilted and formal note, perhaps because she was dreadfully afraid of herself when she wrote it. She told him about the boy Kirk Abbott whom she was going to marry that summer and she explained to Homer how impossible it would have been for them to try and go on with the beautiful but unfortunate thing that had happened to them last night in the field.

She saw him only once after that. She saw him walking across the campus with his friend Hertha, the tall, weedy girl who wore thick-lensed glasses. Hertha was clinging to Homer's arm and shaking with outlandishly shrill laughter; laughter that could be heard for blocks and yet did not sound like real laughter.

MYRA and Kirk were married in August of that year. Kirk got a job with a telephone company in Poplar Falls and they lived in an efficiency apartment and were reasonably happy together. Myra seldom felt restless any more. She did not write verse. Her life seemed to be perfectly full without it. She wondered sometimes if Homer had kept on with his writing but she never saw any of it in the literary magazines so she supposed it couldn't have amounted to very much after all.

One late spring evening a few years after their marriage Kirk Abbott came home tired from the office hungry for dinner and found a scribbled note under the sugar bowl on the drop-leaf table.

"Driven over to Carsville for just a few hours. Myra."

It was after dark: a soft, moony night.

Myra drove south from the town till she came to an open field. There she parked the car and climbed over the low wooden fence. The field was exactly as she had remembered it. She walked quickly out among the flowers; then suddenly fell to her knees among them, sobbing. She cried for a long time, for nearly an hour, and then she rose to her feet and carefully brushed off her skirt and stockings. Now she felt perfectly calm and in possession of herself once more. She went back to the car. She knew that she would never do such a ridiculous thing as this again, for now she had left the last of her troublesome youth behind her.

# THE NIGHT OF
# THE IGUANA

# THE NIGHT OF
# THE IGUANA

**O**PENING onto the long South verandah of the
Costa Verde hotel near Acapulco were ten sleeping-
rooms, each with a hammock slung outside its screen
door. Only three of these rooms were occupied at the
present time, for it was between the seasons at Acapulco.
The winter season when the resort was more popular
with the cosmopolitan type of foreign tourists had been
over for a couple of months and the summer season
when ordinary Mexican and American vacationists
thronged there had not yet started. The three remaining
guests of the Costa Verde were from the States, and they
included two men who were writers and a Miss Edith
Jelkes who had been an instructor in art at an Episco-

palian girls' school in Mississippi until she had suffered a sort of nervous breakdown and had given up her teaching position for a life of refined vagrancy, made possible by an inherited income of about two hundred dollars a month.

Miss Jelkes was a spinster of thirty with a wistful blond prettiness and a somewhat archaic quality of refinement. She belonged to an historical Southern family of great but now moribund vitality whose latter generations had tended to split into two antithetical types, one in which the libido was pathologically distended and another in which it would seem to be all but dried up. The households were turbulently split and so, fairly often, were the personalities of their inmates. There had been an efflorescence among them of nervous talents and sickness, of drunkards and poets, gifted artists and sexual degenerates, together with fanatically proper and squeamish old ladies of both sexes who were condemned to live beneath the same roof with relatives whom they could only regard as monsters. Edith Jelkes was not strictly one or the other of the two basic types, which made it all the more difficult for her to cultivate any interior poise. She had been lucky enough to channel her somewhat morbid energy into a gift for painting. She painted canvases of an originality that might some day be noted, and in the meantime, since her retirement from teaching, she was combining her painting with travel and trying to evade her neurasthenia through the distraction of making new friends in new places. Perhaps some day she would come out on a kind of triumphant plateau as an artist or as a person or even perhaps as both. There might be a period of five or ten years in her life when she would serenely climb over the lightning-shot clouds of her immaturity and the waiting murk of decline. But perhaps is the right word to use. It would all depend on the next two years or so. For this reason she was particularly needful of sympathetic companionship, and the growing lack of it at the Costa Verde was really dangerous for her.

Miss Jelkes was outwardly such a dainty tea-pot that no one would guess that she could actually boil. She was so delicately made that rings and bracelets were never quite small enough originally to fit her but sections would have to be removed and the bands welded smaller. With her great translucent grey eyes and cloudy blond hair and perpetual look of slightly hurt confusion, she could not pass unnoticed through any group of strangers, and she knew how to dress in accord with her unearthly type. The cloudy blond hair was never without its flower and the throat of her cool white dresses would be set off by some vivid brooch of esoteric design. She loved the dramatic contrast of hot and cold color, the splash of scarlet on snow, which was like a flag of her own unsettled components. Whenever she came into a restaurant or theatre or exhibition gallery, she could hear or imagine that she could hear a little murmurous wave of appreciation. This was important to her, it had come to be one of her necessary comforts. But now that the guests of the Costa Verde had dwindled to herself and the two young writers — no matter how cool and yet vivid her appearance, there was little to comfort her in the way of murmured appreciation. The two young writers were bafflingly indifferent to Miss Jelkes. They barely turned their heads when she strolled onto the front or back verandah where they were lying in hammocks or seated at a table always carrying on a curiously intimate-sounding conversation in tones never loud enough to be satisfactorily overheard by Miss Jelkes, and their responses to her friendly nods and Spanish phrases of greeting were barely distinct enough to pass for politeness.

Miss Jelkes was not at all inured to such off-hand treatment. What had made travel so agreeable to her was the remarkable facility with which she had struck up acquaintances wherever she had gone. She was a good talker, she had a fresh and witty way of observing things. The many places she had been in the last six years had supplied her with a great reservoir of descriptive comment and humorous anecdote, and of course there was always the endless and epic chronicle of the Jelkes to regale people with. Since she had just about the right amount of income to take her to the sort of hotels and *pensions* that are frequented by professional people such as painters and writers or professors on Sabbatical leave, she had never before felt the lack of an appreciative audience. Things being as they were, she realized that the sensible action would be to simply withdraw to the Mexican capital where she had formed so many casual but nice connections among the American colony. Why she did not do this but remained on at the Costa Verde was not altogether clear to herself. Besides the lack of society there were other draw-backs to a continued stay. The food had begun to disagree with her, the Patrona of the hotel was becoming insolent and the service slovenly and her painting was showing signs of nervous distraction. There was every reason to leave, and yet she stayed on.

Miss Jelkes could not help knowing that she was actually conducting a siege of the two young writers, even though the reason for it was still entirely obscure.

She had set up her painting studio on the South verandah of the hotel where the writers worked in the mornings at their portable typewriters with their portable radio going off and on during pauses in their labor, but the comradeship of creation which she had hoped to establish was not forthcoming. Her eyes formed a habit of darting toward the two men as frequently as they did toward what she was painting, but her glances were not returned and her painting went into an irritating decline. She took to using her fingers more than her brushes, smearing and slapping on pigment with an impatient energy that defeated itself. Once in a while she would get up and wander as if absent-mindedly down toward the writers' end of the long verandah, but when she did so, they would stop writing and stare blankly at their papers or into space until she had removed herself from their proximity, and once the younger writer had been so rude as to snatch his paper from the typewriter and turn it face down on the table as if he suspected her of trying to read it over his shoulder.

She had retaliated that evening by complaining to the

Patrona that their portable radio was being played too loudly and too long, that it was keeping her awake at night, which she partially believed to be true, but the transmission of this complaint was not evidenced by any reduction in the volume or duration of the annoyance but by the writers' choice of a table at breakfast, the next morning, at the furthest possible distance from her own.

That day Miss Jelkes packed her luggage, thinking that she would surely withdraw the next morning, but her curiosity about the two writers, especially the older of the two, had now become so obsessive that not only her good sense but her strong natural dignity was being discarded.

Directly below the cliff on which the Costa Verde was planted there was a small private beach for the hotel guests. Because of her extremely fair skin it had been Miss Jelkes' practice to bathe only in the early morning or late afternoon when the glare was diminished. These hours did not coincide with those of the writers who usually swam and sun-bathed between two and six in the afternoon. Miss Jelkes now began to go down to the beach much earlier without admitting to herself that it was for the purpose of espionage. She would now go down to the beach about four o'clock in the afternoon and she would situate herself as close to the two young men as she could manage without being downright brazen. Bits of their background and history had begun to filter through this unsatisfactory contact. It became apparent that the younger of the men, who was about

174

twenty-five, had been married and recently separated from a wife he called Kitty. More from the inflection of voices than the fragmentary sentences that she caught, Miss Jelkes received the impression that he was terribly concerned over some problem which the older man was trying to iron out for him. The younger one's voice would sometimes rise in agitation loudly enough to be overheard quite plainly. He would cry out phrases such as *For God's sake* or *What the Hell are you talking about!* Sometimes his language was so strong that Miss Jelkes winced with embarrassment and he would sometimes pound the wet sand with his palm and hammer it with his heels like a child in a tantrum. The older man's voice would also be lifted briefly. Don't be a fool, he would shout. Then his voice would drop to a low and placating tone. The conversation would fall below the level of audibility once more. It semed that some argument was going on almost interminably between them. Once Miss Jelkes was astonished to see the younger one jump to his feet with an incoherent outcry and start kicking sand directly into the face of his older companion. He did it quite violently and hatefully, but the older man only laughed and grabbed the younger one's feet and restrained them until the youth dropped back beside him, and then they had surprised Miss Jelkes even further by locking their hands together and lying in silence until the incoming tide was lapping over their bodies. Then they had both jumped up, apparently in good humor, and made racing dives in the water.

Because of this troubled youth and wise counsellor air

of their conversations it had at first struck Miss Jelkes, in the beginning of her preoccupation with them, that the younger man might be a war-veteran suffering from shock and that the older one might be a doctor who had brought him down to the Pacific resort while conducting a psychiatric treatment. This was before she discovered the name of the older man, on mail addressed to him. She had instantly recognized the name as one that she had seen time and again on the covers of literary magazines and as the author of a novel that had caused a good deal of controversy a few years ago. It was a novel that dealt with some sensational subject. She had not read it and could not remember what the subject was but the name was associated in her mind with a strongly social kind of writing which had been more in vogue about five years past than it was since the beginning of the war. However the writer was still not more than thirty. He was not good-looking but his face had distinction. There was something a little monkey-like in his face as there frequently is in the faces of serious young writers, a look that reminded Miss Jelkes of a small chimpanzee she had once seen in the corner of his cage at a zoo, just sitting there staring between the bars, while all his fellows were hopping and spinning about on their noisy iron trapeze. She remembered how she had been touched by his solitary position and lack-lustre eyes. She had wanted to give him some peanuts but the elephants had devoured all she had. She had returned to the vendor to buy some more but when she brought them to the chimpanzee's cage, he had evidently succumbed to the general impulse, for now every man Jack of them was hopping and spinning about on the clanking trapeze and not a one of them seemed a bit different from the others. Looking at this writer she felt almost an identical urge to share something with him, but the wish was thwarted again, in this instance by a studious will to ignore her. It was not accidental, the way that he kept his eyes off her. It was the same on the beach as it was on the hotel verandahs.

On the beach he wore next to nothing, a sort of brilliant diaper of printed cotton, twisted about his loins in a fashion that sometimes failed to even approximate decency, but he had a slight and graceful physique and an unconscious ease of movement which made the immodesty less offensive to Miss Jelkes than it was in the case of his friend. The younger man had been an athlete at college and he was massively constructed. His torso was burned the color of an old penny and its emphatic gender still further exclaimed by luxuriant patterns of hair, sunbleached till it shone like masses of crisped and frizzed golden wire. Moreover his regard for propriety was so slight that he would get in and out of his colorful napkin as if he were standing in a private cabana. Miss Jelkes had to acknowledge that he owned a certain sculptural grandeur but the spinsterish side of her nature was still too strong to permit her to feel anything but a squeamish distaste. This reaction of Miss Jelkes was so strong on one occasion that when she had returned to the hotel she went directly to the Patrona to enquire if the younger gentleman could not be persuaded to change clothes in his room or, if this was too much to ask of him, that he might at least keep the dorsal side of his nudity toward the beach. The Patrona was very much interested in the complaint but not in a way that Miss Jelkes had hoped she would be. She laughed immoderately, translating phrases of Miss Jelkes' complaint into idiomatic Spanish, shouted to the waiters and the cook. All of them joined in the laughter and the noise was still going on when Miss Jelkes standing confused and indignant saw the two young men climbing up the hill. She retired quickly to her room on the hammock-verandah but she knew by the reverberating merriment on the other side that the writers were being told, and that all of the Costa Verde was holding her up to undisguised ridicule. She started packing at once, this time not even bothering to fold things neatly into her steamer trunk, and she was badly frightened, so much disturbed that it affected her stomach and the following day she was not well enough to undertake a journey.

It was this following day that the Iguana was caught.

The Iguana is a lizard, two or three feet in length, which the Mexicans regard as suitable for the table. They are not always eaten right after they are caught but being creatures that can survive for quite a while without food or drink, they are often held in captivity for some time before execution. Miss Jelkes had been told that they tasted rather like chicken, which opinion she ascribed to a typically Mexican way of glossing over an unappetizing fact. What bothered her about the Iguana was the inhumanity of its treatment during its interval of captivity. She had seen them outside the huts of villagers, usually hitched to a short pole near the doorway and continually and hopelessly clawing at the dry earth within the orbit of the rope-length, while naked children squatted around it, poking it with sticks in the eyes and mouth.

Now the Patrona's adolescent son had captured one of these Iguanas and had fastened it to the base of a column under the hammock-verandah. Miss Jelkes was not aware of its presence until late the night of the capture. Then she had been disturbed by the scuffling sound it made and had slipped on her dressing-gown and had gone out in the bright moonlight to discover what the sound was caused by. She looked over the rail of the verandah and she saw the Iguana hitched to the base of the column nearest her doorway and making the most pitiful effort to scramble into the bushes just beyond the taut length of its rope. She uttered a little cry of horror as she made this discovery.

The two young writers were lying in hammocks at the other end of the verandah and as usual were carrying on a desultory conversation in tones not loud enough to carry to her bedroom.

Without stopping to think, and with a curious thrill of exultation, Miss Jelkes rushed down to their end of the verandah. As she drew near them she discovered that the two writers were engaged in drinking rum-coco, which is a drink prepared in the shell of a cocoanut by knocking a cap off it with a machete and pouring into the nut a mixture of rum, lemon, sugar and cracked ice.

The drinking had been going on since supper and the floor beneath their two hammocks was littered with bits of white pulp and hairy brown fibre and was so slippery that Miss Jelkes barely kept her footing. The liquid had spilt over their faces, bare throats and chests, giving them an oily lustre, and about their hammocks was hanging a cloud of moist and heavy sweetness. Each had a leg thrown over the edge of the hammock with which he pushed himself lazily back and forth. If Miss Jelkes had been seeing them for the first time, the gross details of the spectacle would have been more than association with a few dissolute members of the Jelkes family had prepared her to stomach, and she would have scrupulously avoided a second glance at them. But Miss Jelkes had been changing more than she was aware of during this period of preoccupation with the two writers, her scruples were more undermined than she suspected, so that if the word *pigs* flashed through her mind for a moment, it failed to distract her even momentarily from what she was bent on doing. It was a form of hysteria that had taken hold of her, her action and her speech were without volition.

"Do you know what has happened!" she gasped as she came toward them. She came nearer than she would have consciously dared, so that she was standing directly over the young writer's prone figure. "That horrible boy, the son of the Patrona, has tied up an Iguana beneath my bedroom. I heard him tying it up but I didn't know what it was. I've been listening to it for hours, ever since supper, and didn't know what it was. Just now I got up to investigate, I looked over the edge of the verandah and there it was, scuffling around at the end of its little rope!"

Neither of the writers said anything for a moment, but the older one had propped himself up a little to stare at Miss Jelkes.

"There *what* was?" he enquired.

"She is talking about the Iguana," said the younger.

"Oh! Well, what about it?"

"How can I sleep?" cried Miss Jelkes. "How could anyone sleep with that example of Indian savagery right underneath my door!"

"You have an aversion to lizards?" suggested the older writer.

"I have an aversion to brutality!" corrected Miss Jelkes.

"But the lizard is a very low grade of animal life. Isn't it a very low grade of animal life?" he asked his companion.

"Not as low as some," said the younger writer. He was grinning maliciously at Miss Jelkes, but she did not notice him at all, her attention was fixed upon the older writer.

"At any rate," said the writer, "I don't believe it is capable of feeling half as badly over its misfortune as you seem to be feeling for it."

"I don't agree with you," said Miss Jelkes. "I don't agree with you at all! We like to think that we are the only ones that are capable of suffering but that is just human conceit. We are not the only ones that are capable of suffering. Why, even plants have sensory impressions. I have seen some that closed their leaves when you touched them!"

She held out her hand and drew her slender fingers into a chalice that closed. As she did this she drew a deep, tortured breath with her lips pursed and nostrils flaring and her eyes rolled heavenwards so that she looked like a female Saint on the rack.

The younger man chuckled but the older one continued to stare at her gravely.

"I am sure," she went on, "that the Iguana has very definite feelings, and you would be, too, if you had been listening to it, scuffling around out there in that awful dry dust, trying to reach the bushes with that rope twisted about its neck, making it almost impossible for it to breathe!"

She clutched her throat as she spoke and with the other hand made a clawing gesture in the air. The younger writer broke into a laugh, the older one smiled at Miss Jelkes.

"You have a real gift," he said, "for vicarious experience."

"Well, I just can't stand to witness suffering," said Miss Jelkes. "I can endure it myself but I just can't stand to witness it in others, no matter whether it's human suffering or animal suffering. And there is so much suffering in the world, so much that is necessary suffering, such as illnesses and accidents which cannot be avoided. But there is so much unnecessary suffering, too, so much that is inflicted simply because some people have a callous disregard for the feelings of others. Sometimes it almost seems as if the universe was designed by the Marquis de Sade!"

She threw back her head with an hysterical laugh.

"And I do not believe in the principle of atonement," she went on. "Isn't it awful, isn't it really preposterous that practically all our religions should be based on the principle of atonement when there is really and truly no such thing as guilt?"

"I am sorry," said the older writer. He rubbed his forehead. "I am not in any condition to talk about God."

"Oh, I'm not talking about God," said Miss Jelkes. "I'm talking about the Iguana!"

"She's trying to say that the Iguana is one of God's creatures," said the younger writer.

"But that one of God's creatures," said the older, "is now in the possession of the Patrona's son!"

"That one of God's creatures," Miss Jelkes exclaimed, "is now hitched to a post right underneath my door, and late as it is I have a very good notion to go and wake up the Patrona and tell her that they have got to turn it loose or at least to remove it some place where I can't hear it!"

The younger writer was now laughing with drunken vehemence. "What are you bellowing over?" the older one asked him.

"If she goes and wakes up the Patrona, anything can happen!"

"What?" asked Miss Jelkes. She glanced uncertainly at both of them.

"That's quite true," said the older. "One thing these Mexicans will not tolerate is the interruption of sleep!"

"But what can she do but apologize and remove it!" demanded Miss Jelkes. "Because after all, it's a pretty outrageous thing to hitch a lizard beneath a woman's door and expect her to sleep with that noise going on all night!"

"It might not go on all night," said the older writer.

"What's going to stop it?" asked Miss Jelkes.

"The Iguana might go to sleep."

"Never!" said Miss Jelkes. "The creature is frantic and what it is going through must be a nightmare!"

"You're bothered a good deal by noises?" asked the older writer. This was, of course, a dig at Miss Jelkes for her complaint about the radio. She recognized it as such and welcomed the chance it gave to defend and explain. In fact this struck her as being the golden moment for breaking all barriers down.

"That's true, I am!" she admitted breathlessly. "You see, I had a nervous breakdown a few years ago, and while I'm ever so much better than I was, sleep is more necessary to me than it is to people who haven't gone through a terrible thing like that. Why, for months and months I wasn't able to sleep without a sedative tablet, sometimes two of them a night! Now I hate like anything to be a nuisance to people, to make unreasonable demands, because I am always so anxious to get along well with people, not only peaceably, but really *cordially* with them — even with strangers that I barely *speak* to — However it sometimes happens..."

She paused for a moment. A wonderful thought had struck her.

"I know what I'll do!" she cried out. She gave the older writer a radiant smile.

"What's that?" asked the younger. His tone was full of suspicion but Miss Jelkes smiled at him, too.

"Why, I'll just move!" she said.

"Out of the Costa Verde?" suggested the younger.

"Oh, no, no, no! No, indeed! It's the nicest resort hotel I've ever stopped at! I mean that I'll change my room."

"Where will you change it to?"

"Down here," said Miss Jelkes, "to this end of the verandah! I won't even wait till morning. I'll move right now. All these vacant rooms, there couldn't be any objection, and if there is, why, I'll just explain how totally impossible it was for me to sleep with that lizard's commotion all night!"

She turned quickly about on her heels, so quickly that she nearly toppled over on the slippery floor, caught her breath laughingly and rushed back to her bedroom. Blindly she swept up a few of her belongings in her arms and rushed back to the writers' end of the verandah where they were holding a whispered consultation.

"Which is your room?" she asked.

"We have two rooms," said the younger writer coldly.

"Yes, one each," said the older.

"Oh, of course!" said Miss Jelkes. "But I don't want to make the embarrassing error of confiscating one of you gentlemen's beds!"

She laughed gaily at this. It was the sort of remark she would make to show new acquaintances how far from being formal and prudish she was. But the writers were not inclined to laugh with her, so she cleared her throat and started blindly toward the nearest door, dropping a comb and a mirror as she did so.

"Seven years bad luck!" said the younger man.

"It isn't broken!" she gasped.

"Will you help me?" she asked the older writer.

He got up unsteadily and put the dropped articles back on the disorderly pile in her arms.

"I'm sorry to be so much trouble!" she gasped pathetically. Then she turned again to the nearest doorway.

"Is this one vacant?"

"No, that's mine," said the younger.

"Then how about *this* one?"

"That one is mine," said the older.

"Sounds like the Three Bears and Goldilocks!" laughed Miss Jelkes. "Well, oh, dear — I guess I'll just have to take *this* one!"

She rushed to the screen door on the other side of the younger writer's room, excitingly aware as she did so that this would put her within close range of their nightly conversations, the mystery of which had tantalized her for weeks. Now she would be able to hear every word that passed between them unless they actually whispered in each other's ear!

She rushed into the bedroom and let the screen door slam.

She switched on the suspended light bulb and hastily

plunged the articles borne with her about a room that was identical with the one that she had left and then plopped herself down upon an identical white iron bed.

There was silence on the verandah.

Without rising she reached above her to pull the cord of the light-bulb. Its watery yellow glow was replaced by the crisp white flood of moonlight through the gauze-netted window and through the screen of the door.

She lay flat on her back with her arms lying rigidly along her sides and every nerve tingling with excitement over the spontaneous execution of a piece of strategy carried out more expertly than it would have been after days of preparation.

For a while the silence outside her new room continued.

Then the voice of the younger writer pronounced the word "Goldilocks!"

Two shouts of laughter rose from the verandah. It continued without restraint till Miss Jelkes could feel her ears burning in the dark as if rays of intense light were concentrated on them.

There was no more talk that evening, but she heard their feet scraping as they got off the hammocks and walked across the verandah to the further steps and down them.

Miss Jelkes was badly hurt, worse than she had been hurt the previous afternoon, when she had complained about the young man's immodesty on the beach. As she lay there upon the severe white bed that smelled of ammonia she could feel coming toward her one of those annihilating spells of neurasthenia which had led to her breakdown six years ago. She was too weak to cope with it, it would have its way with her and bring her God knows how close to the verge of lunacy and even possibly over! What an intolerable burden, and why did she have to bear it, she who was so humane and gentle by nature that even the sufferings of a lizard could hurt her! She turned her face to the cold white pillow and wept. She wished that she were a writer. If she were a writer it would be possible to say things that only Picasso had ever put into paint. But if she said them, would anybody believe them? Was her sense of the enormous grotesquerie of the world communicable to any other person? And why should it be told if it could be? And why, most of all, did she make such a fool of herself in her frantic need to find some comfort in people!

She felt that the morning was going to be pitilessly hot and bright and she turned over in her mind the list of neuroses that might fasten upon her. Everything that is thoughtless and automatic in healthy organisms might take on for her an air of preposterous novelty. The act of breathing and the beat of her heart and the very process of thinking would be self-conscious if this worst-of-all neuroses should take hold of her — and take hold of her it would, because she was so afraid of it! The precarious balance of her nerves would be all overthrown. Her entire being would turn into a feverish little machine for the production of fears, fears that could not be put into words because of their all-encompassing immensity, and even supposing that they could be put into language and so be susceptible to the comfort of telling — who was there at the Costa Verde, this shadowless rock by the ocean, that she could turn to except the two young writers who seemed to despise her? How awful to be at the mercy of merciless people!

Now I'm indulging in self-pity, she thought.

She turned on her side and fished among articles on the bed-table for the little cardboard box of sedative tablets. They would get her through the night, but to-morrow — oh, tomorrow! She lay there senselessly crying, hearing even at this distance the efforts of the captive Iguana to break from its rope and scramble into the bushes....

II

WHEN Miss Jelkes awoke it was still a while before morning. The moon, however, had disappeared from the sky and she was lying in blackness that would have been total except for tiny cracks of light that came through the wall of the adjoining bedroom, the one that was occupied by the younger writer.

It did not take her long to discover that the younger writer was not alone in his room. There was no speech but the quality of sounds that came at intervals through the partition made her certain the room had two people in it.

If she could have risen from bed and peered through one of the cracks without betraying herself she might have done so, but knowing that any move would be overheard, she remained on the bed and her mind was now alert with suspicions which had before been only a formless wonder.

At last she heard someone speak.

"You'd better turn out the light," said the voice of the younger writer.

"Why?"

"There are cracks in the wall."

"So much the better. I'm sure that's why she moved down here."

The younger one raised his voice.

"You don't think she moved because of the Iguana?"

"Hell, no, that was just an excuse. Didn't you notice how pleased she was with herself, as if she had pulled off something downright brilliant?"

"I bet she's eavesdropping on us right this minute," said the younger.

"Undoubtedly she is. But what can she do about it?"

"Go to the Patrona."

Both of them laughed.

"The Patrona wants to get rid of her," said the younger.

"Does she?"

"Yep. She's crazy to have her move out. She's even given the cook instructions to put too much salt in her food."

They both laughed.

Miss Jelkes discovered that she had risen from the bed. She was standing uncertainly on the cold floor for a moment and then she was rushing out of the screen door and up to the door of the younger writer's bedroom.

She knocked on the door, carefully keeping her eyes away from the lighted interior.

"Come in," said a voice.

"I'd rather not," said Miss Jelkes. "Will you come here for a minute?"

"Sure," said the younger writer. He stepped to the door, wearing only the trousers to his pyjamas.

"Oh," he said. "It's you!"

She stared at him without any idea of what she had come to say or had hoped to accomplish.

"Well?" he demanded brutally.

"I — I heard you!" she stammered.

"So?"

"I don't understand it!"

"What?"

"Cruelty! I never could understand it!"

"But you do understand spying, don't you?"

"I wasn't spying!" she cried.

He muttered a shocking word and shoved past her onto the porch.

The older writer called his name: "Mike!" But he only repeated the shocking word more loudly and walked away from them. Miss Jelkes and the older writer faced each other. The violence just past had calmed Miss Jelkes a little. She found herself uncoiling inside and comforting tears beginning to moisten her eyes. Outside the night was changing. A wind had sprung up and the surf that broke on the other side of the land-locked bay called Coleta could now be heard.

"It's going to storm," said the writer.

"Is it? I'm glad!" said Miss Jelkes.

"Won't you come in?"

"I'm not at all properly dressed."

"I'm not either."

"Oh, well—"

She came in. Under the naked light-bulb and without the dark glasses his face looked older and the eyes, which she had not seen before, had a look that often goes with incurable illness.

She noticed that he was looking about for something.

"Tablets," he muttered.

She caught sight of them first, among a litter of papers.

She handed them to him.

"Thank you. Will you have one?"

"I've had one already."

"What kind are yours?"

"Secconal. Yours?"

"Barbital. Are yours good?"

"Wonderful."

"How do they make you feel? Like a water-lily?"

"Yes, like a water-lily on a Chinese lagoon!"

Miss Jelkes laughed with real gaiety but the writer responded only with a faint smile. His attention was drifting away from her again. He stood at the screen door like a worried child awaiting the return of a parent.

"Perhaps I should—"

Her voice faltered. She did not want to leave. She wanted to stay there. She felt herself upon the verge of saying incommunicable things to this man whose singularity was so like her own in many essential respects, but his turned back did not invite her to stay. He shouted the name of his friend. There was no response. The writer turned back from the door with a worried muttering but his attention did not return to Miss Jelkes.

"Your friend —" she faltered.

"Mike?"

"Is he the — right person for you?"

"Mike is helpless and I am always attracted by helpless people."

"But you," she said awkwardly. "How about you? Don't you need somebody's help?"

"The help of God!" said the writer. "Failing that, I have to depend on myself."

"But isn't it possible that with somebody else, somebody with more understanding, more like *yourself*—!"

"You mean *you*?" he asked bluntly.

Miss Jelkes was spared the necessity of answering one way or another, for at that moment a great violence was unleashed outside the screen door. The storm that had hovered uncertainly on the horizon was now plunging toward them. Not continually but in sudden thrusts and withdrawals, like a giant bird lunging up and down on its terrestrial quarry, a bird with immense white wings and beak of godlike fury, the attack was delivered against the jut of rock on which the Costa Verde was planted. Time and again the whole night blanched and trembled, but there was something frustrate in the attack of the storm. It seemed to be one that came from a thwarted will. Otherwise surely the frame structure would have been smashed. But the giant white bird did not know where it was striking. Its beak of fury was blind, or perhaps the beak —

It may have been that Miss Jelkes was right on the verge of divining more about God than a mortal ought to — when suddenly the writer leaned forward and thrust his knees between hers. She noticed that he had removed the towel about him and now was quite naked. She did not have time to wonder nor even to feel much surprise for in the next few moments, and for the first time in her thirty years of pre-ordained spinsterhood, she was enacting a fierce little comedy of defense. He thrust at her like the bird of blind white fury. His one hand attempted to draw up the skirt of her robe while his other tore at the flimsy goods at her bosom. The upper cloth tore. She cried out with pain as the predatory fingers dug into her flesh. But she did not give in. Not she herself resisted but some demon of virginity that occupied her flesh fought off the assailant more furiously than he attacked her. And her demon won, for all at once the man let go of her gown and his fingers released her bruised bosom. A sobbing sound in his throat, he collapsed against her. She felt a wing-like throbbing against her belly, and then a scalding wetness. Then he let go of her altogether. She sank back into her chair which had remained demurely upright throughout the struggle, as unsuitably, as ridiculously, as she herself had maintained her upright position. The man was sobbing. And then the screen door opened and the younger

194

writer came in. Automatically Miss Jelkes freed herself
from the damp embrace of her unsuccessful assailant.

"What is it?" asked the younger writer.

He repeated his question several times, senselessly but
angrily, while he shook his older friend who could not
stop crying.

*I don't belong here,* thought Miss Jelkes, and suiting
action to thought, she slipped quietly out the screen
door. She did not turn back into the room immediately
adjoining but ran down the verandah to the room she
had occupied before. She threw herself onto the bed
which was now as cool as if she had never lain on it.
She was grateful for that and for the abrupt cessation of
fury outside. The white bird had gone away and the
Costa Verde had survived its assault. There was nothing
but the rain now, pattering without much energy, and
the far away sound of the ocean only a little more distinct than it had been before the giant bird struck. She
remembered the Iguana.

Oh, yes, the Iguana! She lay there with ears pricked
for the painful sound of its scuffling, but there was no
sound but the effortless flowing of water. Miss Jelkes
could not contain her curiosity so at last she got out of
bed and looked over the edge of the verandah. She saw
the rope. She saw the whole length of the rope lying
there in a relaxed coil, but not the Iguana. Somehow or
other the creature tied by the rope had gotten away.
Was it an act of God that had effected this deliverance?
Or was it not more reasonable to suppose that only Mike,
the beautiful and helpless and cruel, had cut the Iguana

loose? No matter. No matter who did it, the Iguana was gone, had scrambled back into its native bushes and, oh, how gratefully it must be breathing now! And she was grateful, too, for in some equally mysterious way the strangling rope of her loneliness had also been severed by what had happened tonight on this barren rock above the moaning waters.

Now she was sleepy. But just before falling asleep she remembered and felt again the spot of dampness, now turning cool but still adhering to the flesh of her belly as a light but persistent kiss. Her fingers approached it timidly. They expected to draw back with revulsion but were not so affected. They touched it curiously and even pityingly and did not draw back for a while. *Ah, Life,* she thought to herself and was about to smile at the originality of this thought when darkness lapped over the outward gaze of her mind.

# THE YELLOW BIRD

# THE YELLOW BIRD

<A>A</A>lma was the daughter of a Protestant minister named Increase Tutwiler, the last of a string of Increase Tutwilers who had occupied pulpits since the Reformation came to England. The first American progenitor had settled in Salem, and around him and his wife, Goody Tutwiler, née Woodson, had revolved one of the most sensational of the Salem witch-trials. Goody Tutwiler was cried out against by the Circle Girls, a group of hysterical young ladies of Salem who were thrown into fits whenever a witch came near them. They claimed that Goody Tutwiler afflicted them with pins and needles and made them sign their names in the devil's book quite against their wishes. Also one of them declared that Goody Tutwiler had

appeared to them with a yellow bird which she called by the name of Bobo and which served as interlocutor between herself and the devil to whom she was sworn. The Reverend Tutwiler was so impressed by these accusations, as well as by the fits of the Circle Girls when his wife entered their presence in court, that he himself finally cried out against her and testified that the yellow bird named Bobo had flown into his church one Sabbath and, visible only to himself, had perched on his pulpit and whispered indecent things to him about several younger women in the congregation. Goody Tutwiler was accordingly condemned and hanged, but this was by no means the last of the yellow bird named Bobo. It had manifested itself in one form or another, and its continual nagging had left the Puritan spirit fiercely aglow, from Salem to Hobbs, Arkansas, where the Increase Tutwiler of this story was preaching.

Increase Tutwiler was a long-winded preacher. His wife sat in the front pew of the church with a palm-leaf fan which she would agitate violently when her husband had preached too long for anybody's endurance. But it was not always easy to catch his attention, and Alma, the daughter, would finally have to break into the offertory hymn in order to turn him off. Alma played the organ, the primitive kind of organ that had to be supplied with air by an old Negro operating a pump in a stifling cubicle behind the wall. On one occasion the old Negro had fallen asleep, and no amount of discreet rapping availed to wake him up. The minister's wife had plucked nervously at the strings of her palm-leaf fan till it began to fall to pieces, but without the organ to stop him, Increase Tutwiler ranted on and on, exceeding the two-hour mark. It was by no means a cool summer day, and the interior of the church was yellow oak, a material that made you feel as if you were sitting in the middle of a fried egg.

At last Alma despaired of reviving the Negro and got to her feet. "Papa," she said. But the old man didn't look at her. "Papa," she repeated, but he went right on. The whole congregation was whispering and murmuring. One stout old lady seemed to have collapsed, because two people were fanning her from either side and holding a small bottle to her nostrils. Alma and her mother exchanged desperate glances. The mother half got out of her seat. Alma gave her a signal to remain seated. She picked up the hymn-book and brought it down with such terrific force on the bench that dust and fiber spurted in all directions. The minister stopped short. He turned a dazed look in Alma's direction. "Papa," she said, "it's fifteen minutes after twelve and Henry's asleep and these folks have got to get to dinner, so for the love of God, quit preaching."

Now Alma had the reputation of being a very quiet and shy girl, so this speech was nothing short of sensational. The news of it spread throughout the Delta, for Mr. Tutwiler's sermons had achieved a sort of unhappy fame for many miles about. Perhaps Alma was somewhat pleased and impressed by this little celebration that she was accordingly given on people's tongues the next few months, for she was never quite the same shy girl afterwards. She had not had very much fun out of being a minister's daughter. The boys had steered clear of the rectory, because when they got around there they were exposed to Mr. Tutwiler's inquisitions. A boy and Alma would have no chance to talk in the Tutwiler porch or parlor while the old man was around. He was obsessed with the idea that Alma might get to smoking, which he thought was the initial and, once taken, irretrievable step toward perdition. "If Alma gets to smoking," he told his wife, "I'm going to denounce her from the pulpit and put her out of the house." Every time he said this Alma's mother would scream and go into a faint, as she knew that every girl who is driven out of her father's house goes right into a good-time house. She was unable to conceive of anything in between.

Now Alma was pushing thirty and still unmarried, but about six months after the episode in the church, things really started popping around the minister's house. Alma had gotten to smoking in the attic, and her mother knew about it. Mrs. Tutwiler's hair had been turning slowly gray for a number of years, but after Alma took to smoking in the attic, it turned snow-white almost overnight. Mrs. Tutwiler concealed the terrible knowledge that Alma was smoking in the attic from her husband, and she didn't even dare raise her voice to Alma about it because the old man might hear. All she could do was stuff the attic door around with newspapers. Alma *would* smoke;

she claimed it had gotten a hold on her and she couldn't stop it now. At first she only smoked twice a day, but she began to smoke more as the habit grew on her. Several times the old man had said he smelled smoke in the house, but so far he hadn't dreamed that his daughter would dare take up smoking. But his wife knew he would soon find out about it, and Alma knew he would too. The question was whether Alma cared. Once she came downstairs with a cigarette in her mouth, smoking it, and her mother barely snatched it out of her mouth before the old man saw her. Mrs. Tutwiler went into a faint, but Alma paid no attention to her, just went on out of the house, lit another cigarette, and walked down the street to the drugstore.

It was unavoidable that sooner or later people who had seen Alma smoking outside the house, which she now began to do pretty regularly, would carry the news back to the preacher. There were plenty of old women who were ready and able to do it. They had seen her smoking in the White Star drugstore while she was having her afternoon Coke, puffing on the cigarette between sips of the Coke and carrying on a conversation with the soda-jerk, just like anyone from that set of notorious high school girls that the whole town had been talking about for several generations. So one day the minister came into his wife's bedroom and said to her, "I have been told that Alma has taken to smoking."

His manner was deceptively calm. The wife sensed that this was not an occasion for her to go into a faint, so she didn't. She had to keep her wits about her this time—that is, if she had any left after all she had been through with Alma's smoking.

"Well," she said, "I don't know what to do about it. It's true."

"You know what I've always said," her husband replied. "If Alma gets to smoking, out she goes."

"Do you want her to go into a good-time house?" inquired Mrs. Tutwiler.

"If that's where she's going, she can go," said the preacher, "but not until I've given her something that she'll always remember."

He was waiting for Alma when she came in from her afternoon smoke and Coke at the White Star drugstore. Soon as she walked into the door he gave her a good, hard slap, with the palm of his hand on her mouth, so that her front teeth bit into her lip and it started bleeding. Alma didn't blink an eye, she just drew back her right arm and returned the slap with good measure. She had bought a bottle of something at the drugstore, and while her father stood there, stupefied, watching her, she went upstairs with the mysterious bottle in brown wrapping paper. And when she came back down they saw that she had peroxided her hair and put on lipstick. Alma's mother screamed and went into one of her faints, because it was evident to her that Alma was going right over to one of the good-time houses on Front Street. But all the iron had gone out of the minister's character then. He clung to Alma's arm. He begged and pleaded with her not to go there. Alma lit up a cigarette right there in front of him and said, "Listen here, I'm going to do as I please around here from now on, and I don't want any more interference from you!"

Before this conversation was finished the mother came out of her faint. It was the worst faint she had ever gone into, particularly since nobody had bothered to pick her up off the floor. "Alma," she said weakly, "Alma!" Then she said her husband's name several times, but neither of them paid any attention to her, so she got up without any assistance and began to take a part in the conversation. "Alma," she said, "you can't go out of this house until that hair of yours grows in dark again."

"That's what you think," said Alma.

She put the cigarette back in her mouth and went out the screen door, puffing and drawing on it and breathing smoke out of her nostrils all the way down the front walk and down to the White Star drugstore, where she had another Coke and resumed her conversation with the boy at the soda-counter. His name was Stuff—that was what people called him—and it was he who had suggested to Alma that she would look good as a blonde. He was ten years younger than Alma but he had more girls than pimples.

It was astonishing the way Alma came up fast on the outside in Stuff's affections. With the new blond hair you could hardly call her a dark horse, but she was certainly running away with the field. In two weeks' time after the peroxide she was going steady with Stuff; for Alma was smart enough to know there were plenty of good times to be had outside the good-time houses on Front Street, and Stuff knew that, too. Stuff was not to be in sole possession of her heart. There were other contenders, and Alma could choose among them. She started going out nights as rapidly as she had taken up smoking. She stole the keys to her father's Ford sedan and drove to such near-by towns as Lakewater, Sunset, and Lyons. She picked up men on the highway and went out "juking" with them, making the rounds of the highway drinking places; never got home till three or four in the morning. It was impossible to see how one human constitution could stand up under the strain of so much running around to night places, but Alma had all the vigor that comes from generations of firm believers. It could have gone into anything and made a sensation. Well, that's how it was. There was no stopping her once she got started.

The home situation was indescribably bad. It was generally stated that Alma's mother had suffered a collapse and that her father was spending all his time praying, and there was some degree of truth in both reports. Very little sympathy for Alma came from the older residents of the community. Certain little perfunctory steps were taken to curb the girl's behavior. The father got the car-key out of her pocket one night when she came in drunk and fell asleep on the sofa, but Alma had already had some duplicates of it made. He locked the garage one night. Alma climbed through the window and drove the car straight through the closed door.

"She's lost her mind," said the mother. "It's that hair-bleaching that's done it. It went right through her scalp and now it's affecting her brain."

They sat up all that night waiting for her, but she didn't come home. She had run her course in that town, and the next thing they heard from Alma was a card from New Orleans. She had got all the way down there. "Don't sit up," she wrote. "I'm gone for good. I'm never coming back."

Six years later Alma was a character in the old French Quarter of New Orleans. She hung out mostly on "Monkey-Wrench Corner" and picked up men around there. It was certainly not necessary to go into a good-time house to have a good time in the Quarter, and it hadn't taken her long to find that out. It might have seemed to some people that Alma was living a wasteful and profligate existence, but if the penalty for it was death, well, she was a long time dying. In fact she seemed to prosper on her new life. It apparently did not have a dissipating effect on her. She took pretty good care of herself so that it wouldn't, eating well and drinking just enough to be happy. Her face had a bright and innocent look in the mornings, and even when she was alone in her room it sometimes seemed as if she weren't alone—as if someone were with her, a disembodied someone, perhaps a remote ancestor of liberal tendencies who had been displeased by the channel his blood had taken till Alma kicked over the traces and jumped right back to the plumed-hat cavaliers.

Of course, her parents never came near her again, but once they dispatched as emissary a young married woman they trusted.

The woman called on Alma in her miserable little furnished room—or crib, as it actually was—on the shabbiest block of Bourbon Street in the Quarter.

"How do you live?" asked the woman.

"What?" said Alma, innocently.

"I mean how do you get along?"

"Oh," said Alma, "people give me things."

"You mean you accept gifts from them?"

"Yes, on a give-and-take basis," Alma told her.

The woman looked around her. The bed was unmade and looked as if it had been that way for weeks. The two-burner stove was loaded with unwashed pots in some of which grew a pale fungus. Tickets from pawnshops were stuck round the edge of the mirror along with many, many photographs of young men, some splitting their faces with enormous grins while others stared softly at space.

"These photographs," said the woman, "are these—are these your friends?"

"Yes," said Alma, with a happy smile. "Friends and acquaintances, strangers that pass in the night!"

"Well, I'm not going to mention this to your father!"

"Oh, go on and tell the old stick-in-the-mud," said Alma. She lit a cigarette and blew the smoke at her caller.

The woman looked around once more and noticed that the doors of the big armoire hung open on white summer dresses that were covered with grass stains.

"You go on picnics?" she asked.

"Yes, but not church ones," said Alma.

The woman tried to think of something more to ask but she was not gifted with an agile mind, and Alma's attitude was not encouraging.

"Well," she said finally, "I had better be going."

"Hurry back," said Alma, without getting up or looking in the woman's direction.

Shortly thereafter Alma discovered that she was becoming a mother.

She bore a child, a male one, and not knowing who was the father, she named it John after the lover that she had liked best, a man now dead. The son was perfect, very blond and glowing, a lusty infant.

Now from this point on the story takes a strange turn that may be highly disagreeable to some readers, if any still hoped it was going to avoid the fantastic.

This child of Alma's would have been hanged in Salem. If the Circle Girls had not cried out against Alma (which they certainly would have done), they would have gone into fifty screaming fits over Alma's boy.

He was thoroughly bewitched. At half-past six every morning he crawled out of the house and late in the evening he returned with fists full of gold and jewels that smelled of the sea.

Alma grew very rich indeed. She and the child went North. The child grew up in a perfectly normal way to youth and to young manhood, and then he no longer crawled out and brought back riches. In fact that old habit seemed to have slipped his mind somehow, and no mention was ever made of it. Though he and his mother did not pay much attention to each other, there was a great and silent respect between them while each went about his business.

When Alma's time came to die, she lay on the bed and wished her son would come home, for lately the son had gone on a long sea-voyage for unexplained reasons. And while she was waiting, while she lay there dying, the bed began to rock like a ship on the ocean, and all at once not John the Second, but John the First appeared, like Neptune out of the ocean. He bore a cornucopia that was dripping with seaweed and his bare chest and legs had acquired a greenish patina such as a bronze statue comes to be covered with. Over the bed he emptied his horn of plenty which had been stuffed with treasure from wrecked Spanish galleons: rubies, emeralds, diamonds, rings, and necklaces of rare gold, and great loops of pearls with the slime of the sea clinging to them.

"Some people," he said, "don't even die empty-handed."

And off he went, and Alma went off with him.

The fortune was left to The Home For Reckless Spenders. And in due time the son, the sailor, came home, and a monument was put up. It was a curious thing, this monument. It showed three figures of indeterminate gender astride a leaping dolphin. One bore a crucifix, one a cornucopia, and one a Grecian lyre. On the side of the plunging fish, the arrogant dolphin, was a name inscribed, the odd name of Bobo, which was the name of the small yellow bird that the devil and Goody Tutwiler had used as a go-between in their machinations.

# Some New Directions Paperbooks

For complete listing request complete catalog from
New Directions, 80 Eighth Avenue, New York 10011

† Bilingual